DO-IT YOURSELF
DREAM
HUNTS

Mike Schoby

Plan Like an Outfitter & Hunt for Less

©2008 Michael Schoby

Published by

krause publications

An Imprint of F+W Publications

700 East State Street • Iola, WI 54990-0001
715-445-2214 • 888-457-2873
www.krausebooks.com

Our toll-free number to place an order or obtain
a free catalog is (800) 258-0929.

Library of Congress Control Number: 2007936904

ISBN-13: 978-0-89689-641-3
ISBN-10: 0-89689-641-2

Designed by Kara Grundman
Edited by Derrek Sigler

Printed in China

Dedication

To my parents for starting me down the path.
To Dory for tolerating it.

Table Of Contents

Foreword

by Michael Waddell

To many people, I am often thought of as a "TV personality," a person who makes his living off the outdoors, someone who hunts full time, or as a "prostaff" adviser to outdoor companies. But behind the cameras, the "industry" and the persona, there is just plain old huntin'. Nothing but me, a rifle, a huntin' license and my granpapa's old farm. To those that truly know me, I am just a hunter, albeit a passionately addicted one, but no different than you.

Hunting and the celebration of hunting is my life, and has been a constant force since I was old enough to walk behind my papa. Growing up in the rural south, at an early age I realized that there was something about hunting that made it more than a pastime or a hobby, but a lifestyle… an obsession… a passion. It had a tremendous pull on me no different than it does on millions of other Americans.

My father was, and still is, likewise tore up by hunting. Yes, he hunted to put food on the table, but as I watched him during my youth it became evident that he hunted for more than food for the stomach, but food for his soul. He was motivated by the experience, the excitement and the plain old adrenalin rush that follows one of the many magnificent sights that only Mother Nature can provide. Hunting was his lifeblood that he would no sooner deny as he would air, or water. Nature had a pull on him as strong as anything else in the world.

As I grew older It was only natural that I yearned to hunt more places for more species than what was found on the family farm. While I still love giving an ole freak nasty whitetail a permanent parking ticket, the dream of elk bugling in the Rocky Mountains, bowhunting moose in the Alaskan wilderness like Fred Bear and stalking caribou across the frozen tundra all started to occupy more and more space in my mind.

But like most Americans, when it came to hunting I had champagne dreams on a Bud Light budget! Even when we started the television show **Realtree Roadtrips**, it was not an immediate answer to my big game hunting dreams. Yeah, we had a show, and we got to "do what we wanted" but only within the limited constraints of what we could afford and in the beginning this wasn't much! We filmed a lot of our first trips at places we could drive to from Georgia and hunted what ever we could find. That meant a lot of coons, squirrels and turkeys for the first few seasons.

So I know all about limited budgets and big dreams. Through the course of my career I have had the chance to celebrate the hunt with sportsmen from all over the country and for many of them big game, game bigger than whitetails, is just a dream. Unfortunately many think it is an unobtainable one. It is fitting that this book is titled Dream Hunts as most species in America can be transformed from a dream to a reality – and this book shows you how.

Since my early dreamin' years I have had the opportunity to chase those beautiful, dark horned caribou of the North. I have ridden a horse for what seemed like weeks to put an arrow into a mountain of a moose in Alaska. I have taken bears all over the place and along the way even managed to play some string music to some magnificent elk buglin' and I have to say that the reality of the actual hunt has been as good, if not better than the dreams.

Hunting big game doesn't have to be expensive either – you can hunt all across our wonderful country on the cheap if you have the desire and can be a little creative. The lodging may be rough, the hunting may be physically demanding, and you may not always be successful, but the experience will be priceless and along the way you will forge irreplaceable memories and discover true, proven friends.

When it is all said and done, no matter who you are or where you live you can always find a piece of land, buy a tag and we can all celebrate the hunt together regardless of the actual species. If you have ever dreamed of hunting big game in North American it is time to take the next step and start putting your own road trip together today.

Introduction

L ike the vast majority of Americans I grew up in a middle class family. My father had a "normal" office job in the city, but came from farming lineage. Growing up in 1950's rural America he, like many others of his generation, had developed a passion for the outdoors that he carried with him through life. Strongly believing in passing this tradition on, for my 7th birthday I got probably the most life-changing gift I ever will receive – a Daisy Red Rider BB gun. That gun, combined with a near manically obsession for any and all outdoor literature sparked in me the dream of hunting big game.

While I would daydream of hunting any and all sorts of big game, for the most part my dreams changed with the books I read. When I discovered Jack O'Conner, my overactive imagination put me alongside him on various mule deer and sheep hunts in the arid country of old Mexico and Arizona's Mogollon Rim. And once I got to know O'Conner it wasn't long until his nemesis Elmer Keith popped up. Within weeks of our first introduction I traded my Winchester Model 70 in for an early model Smith and Wesson and spurred my mental horse to Salmon, Idaho to chase elk in the high country. After a brief stint with a handgun I decided to challenge my imagination even more with a recurve bow and headed north to Alaska with Fred Bear for brown bears. When the Alaskan climate wore thin I jumped a steamer to warmer locales with Capstick and Ruark where I bagged four of the big five on a 30 day imaginary lorry safari into the Northern Frontier District of Kenya. I probably would have taken all of the big five and possibly a tusker over a 100 pounds if the damnable Jim Corbet hadn't interrupted with an offer to hunt India for man eating tigers.

Dreams do not have to reside in books alone. If you have the desire, passion and drive to hunt big game, nothing in the world is impossible.

From all of these authors, and their great tales, I learned about big game hunting and I knew in my adolescent brain that as soon as I was an adult I would follow in their footsteps. It was not a question or a dream, in my mind it was a fact in capital letters, as undisputable as God or Christmas. It never occurred to me that most "normal" people considered these type of hunting adventures either:

    a. "out of reach"

    b. "a pipe dream"

    c. "a sport for the wealthy and elite"

I was in my early teens when I really started comparing the base price of an African safari or Alaska bear hunt with my meager minimum wage job pushing a broom. It was then I realize how truly expensive big game hunting could be. I quickly did the math and realized I would have to save every penny I made (literally) over roughly a 10 year period to afford a single one of my dream hunts.

In my dreams money never factored into the equation. However, the realization that money does matter in real life never discouraged me; I made up my mind that I just would have to figure out a way to do it without the means of royalty. The old adage "if there is a will there is a way" was never truer than in my pursuit of big game.

Since then I lived my life by this theory and have experienced big game hunting very few hunters are lucky enough to ever see. I did not strike it rich somewhere along the way, win the lottery, patent an idea or marry a wealthy heiress; I just looked for alternate means and situations to hunt. By doing this I hunted through much of the lower 48 and Alaska, several Canadian provinces, South America, New Zealand and several African countries all before the age of 35. Along the way I had the wonderful opportunity to hunt many of the species and subspecies (with the exception of sheep, but random draw willing, this will happen soon!) found in North America.

My story is not unique, and it shouldn't be. I run into hunters all the time that do not have the supposedly "required" financial means to hunt expensive big game, but have hunting experiences that rival anyone in the world.

These "lucky" hunters all share one trait and it isn't money…it is attitude. Much of successful big game hunting starts with attitude. You have to know you will get to hunt your dream species if you are persistent. Too many hunters today see the prices of guided big game trips and stop looking right there with the attitude of "I'll never be able to afford that!" or "Hunting is going the way of Europe – it is strictly for royalty!"

I say, "Nonsense!" Sure, if you have the means to pay retail for a big game hunt the sky is the limit on what one can spend. There are sheep hunts that cost more than a new, fully loaded pickup, elk hunts that are nearly half of the average American yearly income, and whitetail hunts that cost 20 times what most hunters pay for a new rifle and scope combined.

Unfortunately, if you are like me, the simple fact of the matter is you probably will never be able to afford these hunts – as fun as they would likely be. But I'll tell you something else, you can afford to do a whole host of other big game hunts that may currently seem out of reach and have just as much fun, and more satisfaction doing so.

Ask yourself these questions. Does an elk bugle echoing off the frosty aspen-covered mountainside sound as good if you spent $1,000 to be there instead of $10,000? How about the satisfaction level of putting your tag on a Boone and Crocket whitetail taken on land you found yourself and scouted before the season? Finally while you may only be able to hunt Rocky Mountain big horn sheep once in your life, how exciting will the hunt be after you have dreamed about it, planned it, and made "fake" packing lists for 15 years? It will truly be a once in a lifetime time experience that will never forgotten.

In this book I have outlined many ways to experience some great big game hunting without breaking the bank. But keep in mind not everything is available at a discount. There are just some things in this world that cost money, and in the case of certain big game species, a lot of money and there are no ways around it. In these rare situations, it really just comes down to how bad to you want it?

Bad enough to work a second job? Disciplined enough to save for years? Committed enough to eliminating many of the "wants' from other aspects of your life (such as vacations, golf and dinners out on the town) to achieve it? If you are this committed to big game hunting there is not a legal species in the world that cannot be hunted regardless of income.

This fact recently hit home with me after a backyard conversation with a neighbor and fellow hunter. He is one of the most serious hunters I know, but keeps his hunting mostly to whitetails and waterfowl close to home.

"Yup," he said, "I really want to go on a brown bear hunt in the next year or two, if you can send me some info on some of your outfitters I would appreciate it." This friend of mine is a very experienced hunter, who has also taken many unguided trips out West, but works a normal middle class job and lives a middle class lifestyle, he had no clue how expensive it is to hunt brown bear. I didn't want to have to tell him what a brown bear hunt in Alaska costs – even if I could get him a good deal. At the time I just had received the following year's rates and my outfitters were between $12,000 and $16,000 for a good quality guided brown bear hunt and this is one trip where a "deal" rarely crops up.

Before I could comment my neighbor continued, "I have been saving for about 10 years now and I figure about $16,000 should get a good quality brown bear hunt on the Alaskan peninsula." I was shocked, not only because he knew exactly what a brown bear hunt cost, but was serious enough to have saved up for a decade to do it. If you are serious about doing something, it often takes that kind of dedication to achieve it.

I think H.L. Hunt may have said it best. While he wasn't specifically talking about big game hunting he might as well have been as this quote is exactly spot on.

"Decide what you want, decide what you are willing to exchange for it. Establish your priorities and go to work."

If you truly want to hunt a particular big game species that seems out of reach you need to examine this quote first. If you find you can't make it happen, I would suggest it probably wasn't that high on your priority list in the first place.

The bottom line is, with the right attitude, some hard work and a little creative thinking you too can enjoy the stuff that big game dreams are made of. I hope this book takes you a little further along that path.

CHAPTER 1

Alternatives to High Priced Big Game Hunts

There is little doubt about it; the easiest way to experience successful big game hunting is to book a guided hunt on quality private land. I would be kidding my readers if I said any different. Private land gets only a fraction of the hunting pressure of public land. The folks running the property generally manage the wildlife far better than on public land and the guides and outfitters working the property are in daily contact with the game. Consequently these people have a whole heck of a lot more knowledge regarding the

If you want to harvest trophy animals like this mule deer the author took in southern Colorado you have to go where the animals are, and this generally means limited access either through state draw or private land.

whereabouts of the wildlife than a hunter visiting for their first time for a limited stay. It really is this simple. Hunting large tracts of private land, managed for wildlife, with reduced hunting pressure combined with people who know where the animals are will almost always outweigh plain old luck. And this isn't all just opinion; take a look at the statistics.

Most western states have overall success rates in the low double digits (10-20 percent harvest on average). Guided hunts on quality private land in the same states for the same species are generally better than 85 percent!

But pure success and statistical numbers are not the point of this book. The point of this book is how to hunt big game on a budget and that almost excludes guided private land hunts. For most people they are not affordable. Don't get me wrong, I am not maligning guided hunts. I am all for them, have made them my business and truly believe they are the best option for success for those that can afford them. Later in this chapter I even show how to find some real deals on quality private land guided hunts. But if you can't afford a guided hunt or simply like the challenge of "Doing It Yourself" how can you experienced hunting across North America while stacking the odds in your favor to the best of your ability?

The good news is there is more than one way to skin the proverbial cat, or in this case buck.

GO WHERE THE ANIMALS ARE

A large part of the success of guided hunts on private land is the actual land and this truly is the first key to being successful – finding a piece of land that has an abundance of animals and receives little pressure. It is not that guides have mystical powers over animals or are incredible woodsmen (although some are). They generally know the land very well as they spend a lot of time on it, but much of the time they have a bit of an easier go than the average hunter as the land they are hunting is so much better with a high density of un-spooked game.

Think about it, you can be the best hunter in the world, but if you are trying to score on a trophy class elk in area where there just aren't any, no matter how hard you hunt, at the end of the day the results will still be the same – tag soup. So the first rule of successful hunting is: Hunt where the animals are. This can come through accessing private land without a guide, hunting areas with limited tags available, leasing or managing your own land or by simply putting enough boot leather between yourself and the crowds.

Finding Private Land
Without The Price

Depending upon where you are hunting and for what type of species, access to private land can be obtained in different ways. The most traditional and possibly the most common is by simply asking. Not all ranchers and farmers lease their land to hunting operations. Many, I would say the vast majority either retain the hunting rights for themselves and family or let in hunters who ask. This technique worked a generation ago and can still work today. From my experience the difference from 20 years ago is that gaining permission to hunt by simply asking requires more forethought and planning.

When I first started hunting the West if you saw a piece of ground you wished to hunt you located the landowner (either through the nearest likely looking ranch house or from a Platt map) drove up to the front door, put on your best smile and asked if you could hunt. Often it worked and you were hunting within an hour. If you were smart you would follow up with a "thank you" box of chocolates or a gift basket. This technique still works, but to be honest it is getting harder all the time – especially if you try this during hunting season. A far better method is to scout in the summer and ask a landowner several months in advance. Then communicate with him on when you will come out to hunt once fall rolls around. By staying in touch and offering to come out and help with projects (branding in the spring and fencing in the summer are two very good ways to develop good relationships with local landowners) you stand a far better chance of gaining permission than asking opening day.

Asking to hunt is still by far and large the most economical method of gaining access to private land. However, keep in mind, if the access was as easy to obtain as knocking on the door opening morning, there is a good chance the quality of hunting may be directly related to the time spent in finding the land. Private land that owners allow anyone and everyone to hunt really isn't any different or better than public land. You will be far better off to put the time in, develop a good relationship with the landowner and be one of the chosen few who get to hunt the land.

Trespass Fees

While some landowners still let hunters hunt for free, some in recent years have adopted a "middle road" approach between leasing their land out to an outfitter and just letting anyone walk on. This form of pay hunting is generally referred to as paying a "trespass" or "access" fees. I have seen trespass fees work in several ways from essentially buying access for an entire season, paying a trophy fee per species or just buying access for the day.

Depending on how it is priced and the amount of other hunters on the land, trespass fees may or may not be a good deal. In some instances I like trespass fees because they keep hunters that are really not very serious off the land, but keeps the hunt affordable enough that anyone who is even mildly interested in hunting can afford it. On the flip side, I have also seen landowners ask for trespass fees that rival what a guided hunt would cost, but with no limit on who else is on the ranch nor providing any other amenities such as lodging, guiding, meals, trophy care, etc. In addition to these pitfalls, some landowners charge a trespass fee to access public ground that they have hemmed in with their private ground.

These are my biggest complaints with trespass fees. If I am paying a small amount of money to be there I don't mind if the landowner's son is also out hunting or even other hunters on the same property, but if I have to pay a substantial amount for the privilege to hunt I want the experience to be a good one and not only receive the quality I paid for, but the amenities and service that go along with a steep price.

Some western states (Wyoming is the most notorious for this) are a checkerboard of public and private land divided up in perfect square sections. Some landowners have realized that while their land may not be good to hunt, they can charge hunters who wish to access the public land through their property. In my mind this is criminal and something I have never supported. Western ranchers get much subsidized benefit (from everyone's tax dollars) from public land. They should allow hunters free easement to use the public domain. Public land should be public land. All the lamenting in the world probably won't change this, but I simply choose not to support it

GUIDED HUNTS AT AN AFFORDABLE PRICE

There is no question about it – guided hunts on private land are becoming more and more expensive. While most are not completely out of reach of the average American they have changed the way we look at hunting trips. For example it wasn't that long ago that an avid big game hunter of modest means may have hunted elk every season, now that same hunter may only go on a western hunt once every several years. But when he does, he wants a good chance of coming home with a rack in the back of the pickup.

Going guided is not always a bad option and for certain species in Alaska and Canada, it is the only option. If planned correctly guided hunts may still be affordable.

More and more Americans are required to save for longer periods of time to afford quality guided experiences. Many argue that this is ruining the sport of hunting for the average working class, turning it into something akin to a European nobility pastime. Although it is not as cheap as it used to be, I really don't see this happening. There are plenty of opportunities to go around and too much public land to ever truly drive out the "working man". And while guided big game hunts have gotten more expensive in recent years there are some ways hunters can still find "good deals" that will allow them to take a quality hunt.

When looking for a bargain-priced guided hunt, timing is everything. Forget about trying to find a good deal at a sports show in the middle of the winter. This is really the prime time for outfitters to sell their hunts and deals are a scarce as hen's teeth, regardless of how many "show special" signs you see. Furthermore, if someone is offering up a "good deal" in the prime-booking season, you have to wonder why. The bottom line is not all guided hunts or guides/outfitters are of quality. There is a percentage of them that are just average and some that are just plain horrible. Just because you paid hard earned money for a hunt does not mean it will be good.

Instead of basing your decision on price, decide what you want to hunt, where you want to do it, and how important trophy quality is to you. Then find a guide/outfitter that meets these needs. If he is good, he will be booked up far in advance, and that is fine. He should be. He will also have a long list of past clients as well as several established booking agents working with him. All these critical items are general indicators as to how well he conducts his hunts.

After you have found a good outfitter, find out if he has a list of clients he calls on short notice to fill cancelled spots. Invariably every year a percentage of cancellations occur, and it is no reflection on the outfitter as it happens for a variety of reasons. But when it does, especially at the last minute, it puts an outfitter in a bad situation. He now has a spot open he could have sold for full price to a different client if he had the time to market the trip and the client to plan for it. But now he has a limited window to fill this spot. The price may be reduced because the original client forfeited his deposit or simply because the outfitter is willing to take less. Whatever the reason, if you are flexible, can get out of work, get to the destination and have the cash on hand to spend you can find some real bargains this way. In addition to cancelled hunts, many times outfitters just get an extra allotment of tags they weren't expecting. Like all supply and demand commodities in a free trade economy when there is a surplus of something the price will go down to what the market will bear.

Another great source for finding good deals is to establish a relationship with a large booking agent. Many times booking agents get called first by outfitters to help them move excess inventory. By establishing a relationship with a booking agent and getting on their short list of who they call, you can also get many good deals. By establishing a relationship with a booking agent, not only may you get called first, but will have access to several quality outfitters through one contact.

However, regardless if the special deal is through a booking agent or the guide/outfitter, hunters have to be realistic; discounted trips are rarely "pennies on the dollar." A great deal on a last minute hunt is half off and more commonly the amount is 25%-35% off. Keep this in mind, if you can't afford to pay at least half of the retail price, don't bother getting on cancellation lists as you will only get called once or twice. If you turn the trip down, you generally won't get called in the future.

PUBLIC LAND

We are blessed in America with an abundance of public land in almost every state. This is something hunters in other countries would kill for. No fees, no check-in times, just plain old land you can hunt without asking anyone – it is an "American" experience. For a period of my life, I lived in Africa and even though the Dark Continent is considered a big game hunters dream, the lack of public land was the biggest hunting aspect I missed most. I had plenty of ranches and private tracts of property to hunt, but all required reservations, prior planning and communicating with someone at the ranch. Until you go without the ability to drive to a wooded area, pull out a rifle and a pack and start walking, you don't realize how important it is. The ability to do this, for the most part, simply doesn't exist in many other countries like we know it in America.

It should be obvious that I love large tracts of public land, but there is one problem with it. Depending upon where you hunt, public land can be overrun with hunters, ruining the experience for everyone. The good news is if your big game dreams take you out West, there is

Public land can still provide great hunting opportunities, but you may have to access the backcountry to find them.

more than enough public land to go around. In fact the vast majority of the mountainous states are comprised mainly of "public" land – this may be National Forest, Bureau of Land Management lands, State Wildlife Areas, Wilderness Areas, some parks, National Wildlife Refuges, State funded access areas or even private land generally open to public access, such as large timber company holdings.

Millions upon millions of acres in the United States are open to public hunting, but to truly get the quality hunters are looking for some time and effort are required to find the best public land and avoid the majority of the crowds.

Pressure really comes from two sources; the availability of tags in a region and the degree of difficulty required to access the land. The first part of this equation is easy to manage. Find areas that have lots of public land with limited tag availability. In addition to limited tag availability, look for different seasons when the vast majority of hunters are not hunting. For example I used to hunt a tract of public land along the North Platte River in Nebraska during the bow season. The amount and quality of game was staggering as was the complete lack of hunters. However hunt that spot during the rifle season and it is overrun with hunters and consequently devoid of game (not from being shot off, but being pushed off onto adjacent private land where pressure was minimal).

After avoiding crowds through limited tags/seasons, try to find public land that is hard to physically access. There is a direct correlation between amount of people hunting and the effort required to get there. Most pressure is where access is the easiest. If there is a road near the area you can bet 90% of the pressure will be within a 1-2 mile radius of it. But by pouring over quality maps and mapping software it is easy to see where the remote tracts of country lie. Once this is determined the question arises on how to access it. The first option is by foot. This is obviously the cheapest way to do it, but from a practicality standpoint, if the country is rugged and distances are far, it may not be the best way. It is very difficult getting all the supplies needed into the backcountry for an extended stay and if an animal is taken, getting the meat and trophies back out is harder still. While everyone is different in his or her limitations, I consider about 10 miles one way on foot in rough mountainous terrain my maximum distance if I am hunting solo. I can go farther and for different species will do so, but keep in mind if a large animal is taken you will have to make about 4 trips to get all the meat and camping gear back out. This can make for a very strenuous hunt.

BUSINESS REPLY MAIL

FIRST-CLASS MAIL   PERMIT NO. 318   BIRMINGHAM AL

POSTAGE WILL BE PAID BY ADDRESSEE

Cabela's®
Outfitter Journal
PO Box 1847
BIRMINGHAM, AL 35282-8581

SAVE 68% OFF
the newsstand price

Cabela's
Outfitter Journal

If a hunting area is more than 10 miles from a road other options may be better. In some regions you can organize a boat trip on a river or lake. This is a very comfortable way of hunting as you can bring more than enough gear and have it all with you in a boat. Plenty of food can be brought along with all the makings for a comfortable camp. When a good area is come to, you can set up camp and hunt from there for a couple of days, if animals are not found it is simply a matter of packing up the camp and floating a few more miles. The best part of a boat hunt is when you harvest an animal you can pack it downhill to the water where it can be loaded into the waiting craft.

If there are no major waterways in the area to boat another option is to hire a string of pack horses. In many parts of the West there are packers for hire that will take you and your equipment into the backcountry. Generally they work in a set region and know where the various good camping and hunting spots are. While every arrangement is different most of the time they will bring you and your gear in and then come back at a certain time to get your gear and what ever game you have back out to civilization. I have had mixed results with pack trips and go into more details on further chapters about their pros and cons.

Flying in to the back country is not just done in Alaska. Several western states have air taxi services that transport hunters deep into the backcountry. Depending upon the hunt, this can be a great way to get away from crowds and is not as expensive as many would think.

Flying (while more expensive) may be another option. Bush planes are thought of mainly in regards to Alaska and Canada, but many remote Rocky Mountain regions have small bush plane services. Usually utilizing Super Cubs, Huskies, Maules and Cessnas which are perfectly equipped to land on rough gravel bars, wilderness strips and watercourses, these light aircraft make an ideal solution for accessing remote regions. Rented by the amount of gear needed to transport and the distance to the landing area, they will not be cheap, but are very convenient. These air charter services will drop you and your gear off and will come back at a predetermined time to pick you up. The only hang up with light aircraft can be weather. The old bush pilot adage of "if you got time to spare, go by air" is especially true when it comes to mountain flying in the fall and winter. Clouds, rain, wind and snow can shut this service down and hunters need to be prepared with emergency rations to stay in camp for extra days in case the plane can't get back in until the weather breaks. While this is the exception rather than the rule, I have a guide friend who got stuck on a high mountain lake in Alaska for 27 days on a late season mountain goat hunt before being picked up. Luckily he had adequate emergency rations, plenty of fuel, and he ate most of the goat meat before he could be picked up. But he made it.

MILITARY BASES

Military bases can sometimes provide a unique public hunting opportunity. Most of them are generally open to hunting, but may require some kind of special instructional class and the portion of the base that is open to hunting may change frequently depending upon current military training maneuvers. Most bases also require some kind of check-in and check-out policy. For these reason it has been my experience that they are not hunted nearly as heavily as other public spots and can offer some exceptional opportunities for trophy game. If there is a large military base in the region you are planning on hunting, be sure to check in with them well before season as often special classes will needed to be taken in advance to access the property.

PARKS

Depending on the type of park and the state, many hunters are surprised to find out that some of them allow hunting. Generally park hunting is not done with the intent of increasing hunter access, but to control animal populations. That being said parks, especially in the

Some parks may permit limited hunting options, while not always a given it may be a worthwhile hot spot to look into.

Midwest, can be a real sleeper spot for trophy whitetails. Check on state web pages for more information, sometimes you even have to call the particular park to get the straight scoop on what is allowed.

While not generally considered "parks" in the truest sense, "city hunts" kind of fall into this same category. As an example, a small town or city may have a deer overpopulation problem and turn to hunting to manage the herd. You really have to be on top of an area and the politics of that area to find out about these hunts. Generally, you'll have to follow some very specific regulations and take classes in order to participate, but the results can definitely be worth it.

LEASING LAND

Leasing your own private honey hole has become more common in recent years and with good reason. It assures you a private piece of ground to hunt that you can self manage the amount of pressure and control, to some extent, the quality of game. There is no doubt about it, from the South to the North and from coast to coast; leasing land for recreational purposes is becoming common practice. Leases structures are as varied as the hunters who do them, so there is no one set way to lease land. Leases may range from short term, (generally season to season) to long term (generally from one year to several). They may include all species or just a certain species. They may allow the landowner to retain hunting rights for himself and immediate family or they may be totally exclusive. They may be solely for one person with no one else allowed or have the ability to be purchased by a group with decision making rights to allow guests or not. And in more recent years there are even ultra short-term leases, which are just for specific week or segment of the season. "These ultra short leases are ideal for hunters looking to access some prime country at a fraction of the cost," says Pat Gaffney, Owner of RAM Land Management, a company that brokers hunting leases.

In addition to firms like RAM Land Management that specializes in leasing property, leases can originate from private landowners, corporate landowners and even large tract landowners like timber companies subdividing their property for recreational leases. A lease may include just the hunting season or it may also be a year around recreational property available for camping, hiking or fishing. The bottom line is leases may or may not include whatever you and a landowner can agree to.

A good lease is a great thing. It allows a hunter much more quality land access than typically can be afforded by any other means (generally a hunter could barely pay the taxes on the property for what a lease normally goes for), gives them exclusive access, allows them to manage the wildlife and allows access to set stands well before season. A poorly designed lease doesn't accomplish any of these goals and generally makes everyone unhappy – much like a bad timeshare or marriage.

There are formal ways of establishing leases, companies who set them up, as well as many hunters who simply make a proposition to a landowner directly. No matter how you enter into a lease agreement, the important thing is to get all expectations and contingencies in writing well beforehand. It is also not a bad idea to consult with a lawyer before any paperwork is signed. In this light, insurance will need to be purchased as soon as a lease deal is done for the protection of the members as well as the landowner. Most states have a non-lawsuit provision on the books for protecting landowners from litigation arising from allowing hunters access to the property for free, however as soon as money is changed hands this protection goes out the window and all parties may be liable for any accidents/damage that may occur on the property. The bottom line here is, you need to know what the rules are and make sure you're covered.

BUY A PLACE TO HUNT

Buy a place? It is not as far fetched as it sounds. It may be feasible for a hunter or a group of hunters to purchase land for hunting. It takes commitment and some initial investment but may be economically sound in the long term.

Some years ago my father bought an old run down farm in the Midwest. It was sort of an ugly place. There was some waste land, a chunk of scraggly woods and a fair portion of tillable ground. A ravine ran through the middle. The old buildings were a shamble. Very little wildlife was present. The price was right. Over time things started to improve. The buildings were bulldozed which reduced the tax base and cleared more land. Part of the land was entered into the government Conservation Reserve Program (CRP), the rest of the tillable ground was returned to production conducted by a neighbor farmer (automatic food plots and edge cover). A dam was pushed across the ravine to form a very nice private lake. The woods were slightly thinned to remove some scrub brush and leave the young walnuts, oaks, hickories and maples. The brush piles made shelter for the little denizens of the woods.

Wildlife returned with a vengeance. The lake, now stocked with fish, attracted flocks of ducks, geese and a myriad of other critters. Deer and wild turkey showed up. Wood ducks moved into the nesting boxes that were erected. Doves, songbirds and all the lesser wildlife magically returned.

What about the cost? Government agencies helped with the design and construction of the lake. That portion of the expense paid by the owner are tax deductible as a conservation practice. Other conservation projects, such as erosion control, reforestation, and grass waterway construction (more edge cover) are also subsidized and/or tax deductible. Income from farming and CRP payments are enough to cover the taxes and expenses with a moderate excess to clear the mortgage in a reasonable time. A working farm qualifies for several other tax benefits. Interest, property taxes, liability insurance, strip mowing, maintenance of permanent structures (fences, lanes, ditches, etc) are also deductible. All farm deductions are separate and in addition to standard or itemized deductions claimed on ones personal tax return.

The state has a program for registering any untilled land as wildlife area and eliminates the property tax on it. That covers the lake, woods and CRP land. Other states may have similar programs. Improvements and appreciation have increased the land value considerably above the purchase price. Valuable hardwood timber is growing. You could think of it as a pay-for-itself private hunting preserve.

In my youth I could hunt deer elk, bears and a host of small game by simply stepping a short distance from the front lawn of our family home in the Pacific Northwest. I shot my first bear in the garden sweet corn patch. We lived just a very few miles from a major metropolitan center with millions of people. But, our small property adjoined a very large undeveloped area comprised of railroad land, timber company holdings, municipal watershed and National Forest. So, you don't need to own the whole forest. A small place with an old house, cabin or just a place to park a camper will do if it joins or is near a good hunting area. Used as a base of operations, it will greatly increase your hunting opportunities and chances of success. It might even turn out to be a good investment.

SWAPPING HUNTS

Not all trophy hunts come through hard work, expensive leases or guided trips. Sometimes extremely good hunts can and do come from just plain being neighborly. One thing about many hunters is they are gregarious folks who like to share their experiences. It is this sharing that can make for some of the best hunting experiences – not to mention the most affordable.

One of my first serious out of state trips was done this way. I was much younger and while I didn't know Rapid City from Pierre, I knew I wanted to hunt South Dakota. With brush rows full of upland birds, tree groves of fantastic whitetail bucks and Missouri River breaks literally teaming with mule deer, it was a destination that had to be experienced. As it turned out we had a family friend who came from South Dakota and much of his family still farmed some prime country there. After several summer BBQs my father and I were invited to join along on the annual hunt. It was the stuff dreams were made of. Hundreds of pheasants, more than my young mind could quite fathom, deer in every draw and quantities of waterfowl I have only seen since in South America. What did this trip cost? Exactly nothing. Oh sure we chipped in on food and had to buy licenses and get there, but after that it was home cooking, farm house living and Midwest hospitality.

I don't believe I am overly friendly. I have circles of friends and meet people of like interests wherever I go, coincidently those interests are always hunting and fishing. I guess I am just wired that way. If I am at a social gathering of people outside my core group of hunting friends and the group is talking about golfing, skiing or office gossip I am generally not too interested, and will probably be scanning the crowd for the misplaced guy who wore the muddy boots and Carhartt jacket and is looking equally disinterested. Within minutes we will get talking about bucks, fowl or fish and having a great time. Sometimes these occasional encounters turn into a friendship and eventually an invite to their honey hole or them to mine. While this is a very unscientific way of approaching hunting

Look for units with river access as float hunting is often much easier than packing or hiking in. Getting away from the crowds, moving camp and seeing new country is extremely easy when you have watercraft.

it has always worked for me and I have hunted some great land just through networking and contacts.

If meeting people wherever you go is too unscientific for your tastes and would like to take a more formal approach toward finding hunting partners and swapping hunts, there are many other methods available. There are hundreds of online hunting groups, some of which are solely set up for hunt swappers and many more where online communities gather to just swap stories and eventually hunts come out of this. Local hunting and shooting clubs are another great resource, especially if you are new to an area. Not only will they provide contacts for local big game hunting, but there is always a group of guys planning a trip out West or up North and after getting to know the people an invite to come along may be extended.

MANAGING YOUR OWN LAND

Some of the most rewarding hunting comes from managing your own land for trophy animals. While more applicable for whitetails, I have hunted elk, mule deer, blacktail deer and bears all on land our family owned and for the most part managed for wildlife. Planting food plots is the first thing that comes to mind when managing for wildlife and this is a great start as protein rich foods and all season food definitely play a part in growing healthy animals, but managing the male to female ratio, providing escape and edge cover as well as "sanctuary" (non-hunting areas) all play a vital role in managing wildlife. Depending upon the species you are looking to manage you may find out you do or do not have enough land to effectively do so. In the event you don't do what you can and the wildlife will be better off for it. There are many resources available to help you along this path from private organizations such as the Quality Deer Management Association and The National Wild Turkey Federation, specifically their Get in the Game Magazine, to State and Regional Biologists.

THINK OUTSIDE THE BOX

As seen in this Chapter there are many roads that lead to quality trophy big game experiences and not all of them start with shelling out money. There are still many options for big game hunters for virtually any species in America. Some may require more work than others, some require a bit more planning and forethought and others may require a bit of creative thinking, but by thinking out of the box of guided versus unguided it is easy to see there are many options for quality big game hunting.

Sometimes the best hunting can be had by managing your own land for quality. Practicing QDM as well as planting food plots can turn your property into a trophy honey hole.

ENRICHING YOUR LAND ONE STEP AT A TIME

Many folks think that growing their own when it comes to trophy game is as simple as planting a food plot or throwing out a mineral supplement a week before season, but as serious land managers know, growing trophy quality game is a year around ordeal. I spoke with Shane Michelli of Evolved Habitat, a company that produces many wildlife management products such as food plot seed, mineral supplements and protein supplement for game. Most serious land managers plant food plots in the spring and fall that are staggered to provide a viable nutritious food source for most of the year – not just to serve as an attractant during the hunting season.

One of the biggest challenges of hunting the west is getting a tag. Tags can come from over the counter, landowner transferred or drawn. But to get a mule deer like this, getting the right tag in the right area is half the battle. *Photo courtesy of Bob Hadorf.*

CHAPTER 2

Getting a Tag

One of the biggest challenges prospective big game hunters face that they did not have to contend with a generation ago, is the simple act of getting a tag to hunt. As anyone who has looked into big game hunting has discovered, this "simple" act isn't so simple anymore, and this is especially true to hunting in the west.

Much like the coveted animals we seek, acquiring the tag alone today is cause for celebration. In most states getting a tag can require lots of time consuming work, patience, perseverance and a significant investment. The tag situation is a rapidly evolving one with a slippery shifting landscape, but as it is today, here is a general outline of what a hunter can expect when attempting to hunt out West.

Depending upon the state and the specific species, tags can be obtained by one of several methods including, but not limited to: over-the-counter, guide and outfitter sponsored, landowner transferable, state lottery draw, state run raffle, private organization raffle, or auction.

OVER-THE-COUNTER TAGS

This is by far and away the easiest type of license/tag to obtain. As the name implies you can buy these tags over-the-counter much like a small game, bird or fishing license. "Over-the-counter" is essentially the generic term for any method of license that is guaranteed to the general public – it does not matters if the tag is physically purchased over the counter of a retail store, at a Government office, through the mail or online. The common deciding factor is: was the tag available for anyone to purchase? Over-the-counter tags make a hunting trip very easy and convenient to plan as the hardest part of getting there is taken care of.

However, there is a reason for limited access hunts in the first place and many times hunters find out why only after they go on an over-the-counter hunt. Many over-the-counter tag hunts aren't worth the price of admission. Often the quality and quantity of game is poor, or there may be limited public land access meaning nowhere to hunt and nothing to hunt when you get there. If there is a good amount of quality game and lots of access combined with an over-the-counter tag then you will do just as well setting up your tent in a downtown city corner as there will be more hunters than game by opening day. While easy to get, over-the-counter tags are convenient, they are not always a hunter's best choice.

STATE DRAWS

I don't know what state first implemented a random drawing for big game tags, but it is now not only extremely common throughout the West, but making inroads east of the Mississippi for popular trophy whitetail areas, limited moose tags and reintroduced elk herds. Draws can be a very effective tool at managing the number of hunters afield, as well as the number and size of animals taken, but they can also be an incredible pain in the butt and ultimately limit hunter opportunity.

They require yearly diligence to manage and watch, may require a substantial investment in money and will probably take anywhere from two to ten years (or a lifetime in some cases) depending upon the state, species, location, etc. to actually draw a tag.

While every state is different in how they conduct their draw, if you have never participated in one here is a very basic outline on how they work. Begin by researching the state you would like to hunt. Do your homework on which units offer what you are looking for. This may be for a particular species, low hunter pressure through low number of available tags, a particular season for a particular method, or a certain size-class of animal. For the hunter willing to invest the time all of this information is generally available. A great place to start is the state's web site where past draw results including numbers of applicants, and harvest success is usually listed.

After you have determined the exact hunt you are interested in it is pretty straight forward to go about applying. Every state either through their printed material or web site has its procedure and timeline listed for applying for a tag. It may be as simple as filling out the paperwork for the given tag, paying a processing/application fee and waiting to see if you get drawn or it may involve also paying for the cost of the tag upfront, the money to be refunded sometime down the road if you don't get drawn or it may be as costly as purchasing a hunting license for the particular state then applying for the actual tag, the cost of the license is generally forfeited if you don't draw the tag and don't plan on hunting any over-the-counter available species or small game that season. Look to the Western State Roundup chapter in this book where all Western states have a brief description of their draws, tag costs and general information.

If this process hasn't confused the reader enough, add in the sometimes-complicated system of preference or bonus points. Essentially this started as a way to reward non-successful applicants by weighing future draws in their favor and subsequently increasing their odds as years go by. However, even this system changes drastically by state and really may or may not significantly increase your odds and in some cases may severely hurt you if you are just getting into the game of out of state license applying.

For example take a state that has a 10% chance of drawing a particular tag for non-residents i.e. there will be 10 tags given out and 100 people are applying for them. If they have a weighted point system in place this means that the 90 people who didn't draw last year will stand a better chance of drawing a tag than you do (making your actual chances less than the published 10%). If you have been applying from the beginning or have hit maximum bonus points you will start a far greater chance than 10% to draw the same tag. In an attempt to equal out bonus points for new comers some states have capped the number of bonus points people can accumulate, which at first seems like a good idea, but eventually will mean that the odds will be the same without bonus points at all once the bulk of the population all has capped bonus points.

In most states for most species the odds of drawing a particular tag are not very good, many are downright horrible and some are impossible if you don't have bonus points built up. For this reason, many states have opened up a "points only" section of the draw that allows hunters just to apply for points, generally one per year. This allows the hunter to accumulate preference points so when enough are accumulated he can actually start to plan on drawing a tag. When enough points are accumulated the draw odds are improved, then it makes sense to start applying for a specific tag of your dreams.

If applying for specific state/region and species isn't confusion enough, start looking at applying in multiple states or multiple species, and you will quickly discover managing a stock portfolio is child's play compared to this endeavor. But if you are going to be successful at drawing highly coveted trophy tags it must be done. It is a simple equation in statistics. With draw odds being low across the United States you have to take every opportunity you can to increase them. This means getting into more draws. For example if you want to hunt a trophy mule deer unit and you just apply in one state it may take upwards of 10 years to draw that one tag and another ten years to draw a second one. However if you apply in every state that offers a draw for a trophy mule deer unit, after you get enough points built up across the board you could potentially be hunting mule deer somewhere every year. But keep in mind the Devil is in the details. Every state has a different application process and different preference points system (for example some states have a policy if you forget to apply one year you lose all previously accumulated preference points), a different payment system and various deadlines that span over a six-month period.

The best way I have found to manage multiple state draws is to create a file for each state complete with regulations, deadlines, step-by-step procedures on how to apply, past applications, etc and go through it yearly to review each state. While time consuming to set up, once it is done the average hunter should have no trouble managing half dozen states for several species.

State draw systems are generally the most affordable way to hunt where quality animals are without a lot of pressure, but they do come with a price in both yearly fees and lots and lots of personal time.

GUIDE AND OUTFITTER SPONSORED LICENSES AND TAGS

If you wish to increase the odds of drawing a specific tag over the general state draw look at guide and outfitter sponsored tags. There are a few states that offer a guide/outfitter sponsored tag program, and like general state run draws there is really no clear blueprint of what this is as it varies drastically from state to state. However, generally speaking these sponsored programs give hunters who are hunting with a licensed guide or outfitter of that particular state preference over hunters who are going at it solo in the state draw. As previously noted the rules regarding this type of draw vary widely from state to state. In some states the tag is almost guaranteed if the hunter just fills out the paperwork, in some states it is guaranteed, but the license/tags cost a premium to purchase, in other states it just increases your odds, but is not a sure thing. While only a handful of states offer guide/sponsored tags, if you are looking to draw a tag relatively quickly it is something to look into, but keep in mind this generally takes hunts out of the inexpensive category and into the realm of expensive guided hunts.

TRANSFERABLE LANDOWNER TAGS

Transferable landowner tags come in several forms and for the purpose of this subchapter I have listed the many various forms together for easy reading. For all intents and purposes they accomplish the same thing – they allow hunters access to a highly coveted tag without the wait of a lengthy draw, however these tags are often far from being perfect themselves. Depending upon the state, a landowner may be issued big game tags which can then either be transferred with no up charge to a hunter or with an up charge – once again this varies by state. The number of tags allocated by the state varies by the specific program and property size. In some cases hunters are just buying the tag with no land access, other times it comes with a guide or land access. In either case make sure you know what you are getting before jumping in with both feet as these tags are often issued in regions where very little to no public access is available and just having a tag without the land will not improve your chances of harvesting an animal.

Colorado has probably the best method for issuing these tags which they call Ranching for Wildlife tags. Ranches can enroll their property in the program and in turn are granted a certain number of tags for various big game species. These tags are generally very liberal in terms of season and weapon. The ranch then provides these tags to hunters who have booked a guided hunt on their land. While generally not considered inexpensive they are an excellent way of hunting the West during a prime season without the lengthy wait of a draw.

Raffle tags are often long shots at drawing a tag, but sometimes a long shot is better than no shot at all.

State and Private Raffles

Another method of obtaining a coveted big game tag is through state and/or private raffles. For a fundraiser many states will earmark a small percentage of the available tags for a species into a raffle pool. The raffle may be through the state itself, or to a non-profit conservation organization like the Rocky Mountain Elk Foundation, Safari Club International, the Federation for North American Wild Sheep or the like. Depending upon how the raffles are conducted your odds may be significantly better than the general draw and in some cases for a fraction of the price. Take for example the Washington State mountain goat draw versus the state conducted mountain goat raffle. The general draw for a nonresident costs $50 to apply then an additional $1095.50 if you actually drew a tag. The rough odds of this happening in most decent goat units throughout the state are about 1 chance in 469 (in 2006) or another way of putting it, if you apply

By going to a primitive weapon, hunters can often receive tags where rifle hunters wait years for. If you have the patience and skill to get close, bow and muzzleloader hunting is a great way to hunt the West.

every year for 400-500 years you may draw a tag. Compare this to their state draw. Residents and nonresidents alike can buy the same raffle ticket for $5 apiece and buy an unlimited amount. If you invest in 10 tickets (the same amount of dollars spent as the non-resident application fee) your draw odds are roughly 200 and you get the tag for free if you actually win the raffle! While not all raffles are this good, they are worth looking into on a case-by-case basis.

TAG AUCTIONS

Every year there are organizations that raffle off big game tags for various states. This is another option for hunters wishing to hunt certain species in particular places, but for the most part be ready to open you check book. In some cases, certain tags may go for prices that are steep, but still affordable, but most of the time it is like watching a rare item go on the block at Sotheby's - the price jumps by thousands, not hundreds and can reach a couple of times of what an average luxury SUV will cost! Unless you have very deep pockets, auctions are not a viable option for most people. But for certain extremely hard-to-obtain tags, such as bighorn sheep this is one of the few options available to hunters.

THE COST OF DRAWING TAGS

As anyone who has looked at the odds of drawing a big game tag in a coveted trophy region can tell you – the odds are pretty low and the best bet is to apply in several states each year. While this sounds easy enough on paper it may involve a significant cash outlay since in some cases the price of the non-resident tag must be paid at the time of applying. If a hunter is just looking to apply for a deer tag, this can be pretty manageable, but when sheep, goat, elk, moose, antelope,

INCREASING YOUR ODDS BY HUNTING WEAPON

As a general rule the more difficult the hunting method, the easier the tag is to get. Modern centerfire rifle is generally the hardest tag to get, followed by muzzleloader then archery. In many cases even in areas where a rifle tag is nearly impossible to draw, an archery tag can be bought over the counter. Not only will a more primitive weapon tag be easier to obtain, it may also be in a much better time frame i.e. during middle of September for elk, or later fall during the peak of the rut for whitetails or mule deer.

USING A DRAWING SERVICE

There are several companies that offer tag application management services. You provide them with your personal information, what tags you would like to draw and let them take care of the details. In some cases these programs work out very well for hunters who don't want to hassle with the process, but hunters will often have a better idea of their individual needs and are capable of doing it themselves. In the end all of these services have a cost, which can equal a pretty hefty sum over time – which goes against the principle of applying for tags in the first place. If money weren't a concern, it would be much easier to buy transferable landowner tags, sponsored tags or auction tags. Be wary of services that charge a hefty fee per species/state applied (even if they "float" the actual tag cost) for they are significantly more expensive than a service that just charges a membership-style fee with a light per state fee. Remember there is no free lunch and all of the tag application services are in this game to make money. If you want to save money, study the states you are interested in and apply on your own.

deer, audad, oryx, and bison are sought this price can get very costly very fast. While some private application services will "float" the money for their customers until they draw, the hidden costs for this service approach usury rates – avoid these programs like the plague. The good (or bad) news is 95% of the tags applied for will not be drawn and the money will be returned in one to several months. Different hunters have different ways of dealing with this. Some keep a slush fund of money in a savings account specifically used for draws, the money for the tags gets pulled from this account and then redeposit less application and sometimes general license fees if/when they do not draw. Others will put the cost on a credit card if the state allows it. If allowed this a great method as a low interest card over the short duration is one of the most affordable methods of putting in for tags. Whatever method you choose will be dictated by how many states and tags you apply for and your individual financial situation. Just keep in mind for many serious western big game hunters the cost of applying for tags can easily equal thousands of dollars (the majority of which is returned) each year. You will suffer the cost of interest on the money while it's tied up in either case.

Cancellation hunt saves the day

The phone rang. At the other end was a gentleman with a story to tell and need for help.

"It seems that every year for the past few years, I have always ended up moving during hunting season," he said.

"That doesn't sound like much fun," I replied.

"What I'd like to do is go hunting for a few days, but I'm not interested in being guided. I want to be left alone. Do you have anything?"

"I have a cancellation hunt that would be perfect for you," I replied.

And with that, I sent this man and his hunting partner off to hunt with RAM Outfitters at their location near Lacrosse, WI. This had everything these hunters were looking for. The land had tremendous trophy potential with many solid record-book animals taken. It was also 100% fair chase hunting, which was important. The land was scouted and the outfitter placed stands, but the hunters were left on their own.

This corncrib turned hunting lodge was the only point of contact between the hunters and the outfitter. It was a place to get out of the woods and sit down for a snack or just a break from hunting.

The hunter didn't connect with an animal on this hunt, although his hunting partner did. They both had numerous opportunities to do so and things went just like they do when you're hunting. This is a perfect example of how expanding your options and being flexible can salvage a hunting season.

It is also a good example of how looking for things like cancellation hunts from places like Gander Mountain's Outdoor Expeditions can provide great savings on dream hunting adventures and provide the exact kind of hunting you want. These guys didn't want high fences or guides standing over them telling them when to shoot and when not to. Far too often people get the idea that going with a service like this is just for elitists who have money to burn and want to just shoot a big trophy. Such is not the case. The buck these guys ended up with was not a monster. It was a good buck to take and has a unique story behind it, as it was obviously a real scraper. The main point is that they were happy with the deer and the experience.

This buck was sure a scraper. What makes this deer a trophy is the unique rack that obviously has a story behind it. Plus it was a good deer to take from the herd as its injuries might have done him in during the winter. Besides, whatever won the fight was still out there roaming the woods.

CHAPTER 3

Remote Scouting

I believe a generation ago hunters had more time to relax afield. Spending the entire season at deer camp with buddies was a tradition that spanned generations and was looked forward to all year. Today time is at a premium. With the self-induced pressures of a hectic life, hunters are pretty much forced by modern constraints to change the way they scout and subsequently hunt. The world truly is a smaller place and hunters are much more mobile than they were a couple of generations ago. It wasn't that long ago that most hunters spent the majority of their time afield within their home state. A big trip might be to a neighboring state and a trip "out west" might be a once in a lifetime experience. All that has changed, mainly through easily obtained and relatively inexpensive airline tickets, but also through an increased exposure to different hunting destinations through print and televised media. Hunters now think nothing of heading out West for a long weekend. Heck, I even know two guys who flew to Africa for two days of hunting. They got their Cape buffalo, but literally spent more time in the air than they did on the ground.

Hunter looking through binoculars at whitetails.

Combine these factors with an often-higher level of disposable income among today's hunters and you have a mixture conducive for hunters to travel farther from home than ever before. But while hunters' range and tolerance for travel have increased, the amount of time spent afield per trip has decreased. Many Americans spend more time at the job than ever before, have many other commitments on their time and in general live a faster paced life then previous generations. What this all adds up to is American hunters are willing to go long distances in pursuit of game, but generally can't stay nearly as long. I believe these are the main reasons in the rise of popularity of guided hunts.

When hunters don't have the time to scout the area, have invested a lot of money on their only big trip that year they want to come home with an animal. And no matter what else you obtain from this book, remember that a good guided hunt (in terms of sheer success rate) will almost always beat a trip planned and executed by yourself – especially if the trip is a long way from home. The theory is quite simple really. Who knows the region better? Who knows the secret spots and how to access them? Who spends countless days a year watching the animal's movements and who has the landowner contacts and/or the equipment to access the backcountry better – a local guide or a nonresident hunter who may or may not have ever been to the area in question?

I think the answer is pretty evident, but this book is about doing it yourself. Just because you may not have the knowledge and skills of a local guide doesn't mean you have to walk blindly into a hunt. If you want to be successful there are many ways you can and must scout before heading to a remote hunting location.

Scouting is relatively easy if one lives close to the hunting area. It is a simple process to drive out to the area in the evening after work set up a spotting scope and spend a few hours watching for game. It becomes progressively harder the farther it is away. That is not to say it can't be done. It is just harder. By expanding what hunters traditionally think of as "scouting" a lot of information about an area and game population can still be learned regardless of the remoteness of the hunting location. The techniques listed below are all great tools either used individually or better yet in conjunction with each other.

SCOUTING ONLINE

We often lament about the younger generation spending too much time on the internet, but if they are doing the right thing, it might not be all bad. The computer is probably the best scouting/hunt-planning tool ever devised. From the comfort of your own office or home you can access local data on weather conditions, lodging, dinning areas, licensing information, past hunter success of the region, and general size of animals taken as well as converse with local hunters, guides and professional biologists. There is no other tool that can do as much for the non-resident do-it-yourself hunter as the computer. In addition to all these important detail sourcing functions, where it really shines is as an in-depth mapping tool. Today there are programs available that a few short years ago were only available to science fiction writers, NASA and the military. While there are many sites dedicated to mapping, my favorite for online scouting is Google Earth. With a simple download, hunters can access the entire globe right on their computer and access aerial photography anywhere in the world

Computers are the best tool hunters may have at finding trophy areas. From gathering information, looking over the country and meeting fellow hunter, it is hard to beat a computer.

right down to the house/car level. Not only can you zoom in from a birdseye view to see drainages, pinch points, woodlots, natural funnels, saddles etc, you can also rotate the map so you can get a feel of the region's topography from the ground level. While not as useful in flat regions, this is a tremendous help in mountainous country.

In addition to Google Earth, another great source of information is available on many of the mapping software programs used in conjunction with hand held GPS units. The data can be transposed to a hand held GPS unit with the way points already marked so you can easily find your potential hot spots once in the field.

For hunters looking for traditional printed topo maps and aerial photography sites like X, Y and Z all provide excellent maps at a great price.

SCOUTING THROUGH PROFESSIONALS

While the computer is a fantastic tool for doing your hunting homework, there is also the human touch that can make or break a hunt. State and Federal biologists can be a wealth of information when it comes to the area's big game population. These are highly informed, dedicated individuals who more often than not are hunters themselves and spend all their time monitoring the big game in the region. Don't expect to make one call and have them draw a big X on a map to the area's hottest hunting spot, but by developing a long distance relationship over the phone, with follow up letters or emails this can often lead to a wealth of information and some great leads when you finally get to the area. If you are going into an area for the first time or for the tenth, getting to know the local experts can go a long way toward making your hunt a successful one.

SCOUTING BY THE NUMBERS

I like to refer to this method as the "baseball" method of scouting. Like any serious baseball fan that can regurgitate the statistics on batting averages, strikeouts, and RBIs knows baseball is more than a game of chance it is often all about the odds. Even though they know that a game is still a game and anything can happen, the law of averages, and past statistics play a major roll in predicting future performance.

There are a lot of similarities in the hunting world. If the hunter harvest success rate has 5% for a given unit over the last 10 years and there has never been a trophy sized animal harvested in the unit, don't go into the area with high hopes of hanging your tag on a monster. The odds are simply not in your favor. Conversely, if a unit has had a high hunter success rate and the trophy record books show a good percentage of their entries coming from that area you have already set yourself up to have, at least according to the odds, a more successful hunt.

Hunting is still weighed heavily on chance, luck and a hunter's individual skill and effort, but you have to go where the animals are to be successful. Unlike baseball where there are reams of data on every newsstand, there is not this kind of mass information in the hunting world. However, there still is plenty of hunting data for those willing to look for it.

Most state agencies publish their data taken from surveys as well as mandatory game check-in stations in regards to hunter success rates, animal age or size and unit. They also generally publish their data on draw odds and hunter success in specific "trophy" units. Finally, private organizations like Boone and Crocket, Pope and Young and SCI all keep trophy records of big game. Next to the score of the animal state and county list the location of kill. This can go a long way to narrowing down your list of areas with a history of superior quality genetics. Statistics aren't facts. It is possible for the Cubs to win the World Series, everyone also knows it isn't likely. You may find a deer of a lifetime in New York's central park…but your odds are much better to bet on the past proven winning areas.

LEARNING FROM OTHERS MISTAKES

One of the best methods of scouting is talking to other hunters who have hunted the region or better yet the specific unit you are interested in, in recent years. This hunter perspective provides an extremely valuable, in-depth look at what to expect, what the country is like, the number of animals seen and what you should and should not do. Learning from others mistakes is often one of the best methods in life and it pays dividends in the hunting world as well. Internet chat rooms, especially state specific chat rooms (such as those hosted on the particular states game and fish web site) are an excellent source of information that shouldn't be overlooked.

ELECTRONIC SCOUTING

Another great tool for scouting big game animals is using digital game cameras. These cameras came on the market several years ago and have since evolved into relatively economically priced, extremely high quality units. If you haven't used one here is how

The author putting up a game camera.
Using technology like this Stealthcam game camera can maximize your time afield and let you know what size of animals are living in a particular area.

they essentially work. You set them up overlooking a trail, waterhole, food source, field edge – anywhere you would expect to see game. They are triggered by any motion and take from one to several still photos or even short video clips. You can come back several days later, download the images to a computer and hopefully have a better idea of what size class of animals are using the area and when they are using it. For busy hunters this is an invaluable aid. It quickly eliminates areas with few or immature animals and helps hunters focus their attention on areas with significant promise. Like all electronic devices the quality of the technology is rising by the minute. I currently use several Stealthcam remote cameras and am completely satisfied with them, but the industry is always developing new and better versions. Stealthcam's next generation of product will actually send the images via cellular phone to a computer where they can be viewed remotely. This new technology as it becomes refined, and cell coverage expanded, will particularly help hunters scout farther from home.

A trophy buck like this one the author tagged in Kansas comes from good scouting and knowing an animal's habits.

BEING FLEXIBLE

Regardless of how well you do your research and how well you implement your plan there are still many variables that can affect your hunt - a 100 year drought may hit, an early snow storm, a recently published magazine article about the area may send hunters there in droves, a bad winter die off, local hunting pressure, shifting of land from public to private. The best laid plans can and often do go awry. If a hunter isn't flexible so may his dream hunt die. Try to envision all of the factors that may rock the proverbial hunting boat and anticipate recourse. This may mean moving to another area, getting farther into the backcountry, moving to a lower elevation, paying to access private land or changing to a different season or unit all together. You can't anticipate all factors, but try to plan for as many as you can. The more flexibility a hunter can manage the more likely the hunt will come off without a hitch.

Formulating a Plan

After you have done all of your "remote" scouting, you need to compile all the data and formulate a plan. You should be able to narrow down the general area where you want to hunt easily enough by meshing your goals (high success on average-sized game, fair success on trophy-sized game or finding a unit with very little pressure for a great overall experience) with the past performance data from a region. After the general area is determined, next comes the research to select the specific place. This comes from combining all the general data on the region accumulated from various sources with the specific locations found through maps, Internet available aerial photography and local research. At this point you have a good idea or a plan of where to go. Depending upon the actual hunt, how much time and money you have invested, the distance from your home and the difficulty of drawing the tag, you may call this research good enough and wait until the hunt starts to implement your plan. Or you may head to the area for a pre-season-on-the-ground scouting trip. Whichever course of action you take, it is still a plan. You may find out that your plan worked out perfectly, it may need some slight tweaking or it may have to be scrapped all together. That is the nature of hunting, but without a plan you are not stacking the odds in your favor.

The author glasses during a muzzleloader hunt during the last few moments of daylight. Hopefully that buck will still be there come morning.

CHAPTER 4

The Right Tools for the Job

For hunters to be successful on do-it-yourself hunts they need to think, plan and hunt like a guide or outfitter. From firearms and bows to spotting scopes and binoculars, hunters need to be proficient with several tools and have the right equipment at their disposal.

Like it or not, having to select a specific type of sporting arm is a reality of modern big game hunting. Hunters should be proficient with several methods if they want the best opportunities at harvesting game. Most states have several different types of hunting method seasons available and the season as well as the opportunity to hunt varies with the method. In most states, hunters have the opportunity to hunt with archery equipment, modern rifle or muzzleloader. In some cases handguns and crossbows can also be used, but generally speaking there are few special seasons available for these weapons.

ARCHERY

If you love to hunt (imperative word hunt, not kill) there is no better method for the big game hunter than a bow and arrow. There are more opportunities to get outdoors, often with longer seasons that may run through the prime times such as the elk or whitetail rut. Archery tags are often available over-the-counter where tags for other weapons require a competitive draw with very limited success. Finally, almost always there are far fewer people in the woods during the archery season when compared to other seasons.

However, there is no doubt about it; bow hunting has the lowest success rate of all forms of hunting. Even with all of the advancements in modern archery equipment, bow hunting is still really a game of 40 yards or less for most hunters. Just like some riflemen are capable of cleanly taking game past 500 yards, there are some bow hunters who are very proficient past 50 yards, but this

Bow hunting is a great method for all species, western and eastern alike. It generally is easier to obtain archery tags, which offer a better season with far less hunters in the field.

truly is the 1% crowd, for the rest of us, we should stay considerably within 40 yards.

When choosing an archery setup for most big game species, hunters have a lot of choices available today. Starting with the bow, there are many different types and styles available, from recurve and long bows to the highest tech, latest model compound bow. Generally speaking most of today's hunters want moderate speed, pinpoint accuracy and easy maintenance. This is accomplished by almost all modern compound bows regardless of cam type. Depending upon where and how you hunt you may need to be concerned with small technicalities of a bow's riser material, cam design, the overall weight and length. Bows are available for many specialty applications from mountain goat hunting to tree stand perching and everything in between, the advantage of a specialty bow are minimal. For the most part hunters are better off shooting one general bow that does everything pretty well.

Selecting a bow and the accessories to go along with it can be a daunting task, luckily for today's hunters there are many great products on the market to choose from.

Selecting arrows and broadheads is a much more difficult task. For years aluminum arrows have been the mainstay of the big game hunting community, but recently modern wrapped or woven carbon fiber arrow shafts are making significant inroads. They are now very straight, comparable to the best aluminum arrows. They are also very durable, probably more so than aluminum, and are generally lighter which makes for a slightly flatter trajectory. If you feel the advantages are worth it buy carbon, but don't for an instant think that good aluminum arrows will not work. Aluminum arrows have killed nearly everything in the world and work as good today as they did a generation ago. While they are heavier the extra weight means extra penetration and less bow noise due to reduced vibration. Each type of arrow has individual merits, and some may work better in certain situations than others.

There are hundreds of styles of broadheads and each has its own fan base. What style you choose has a lot to do with personal opinion and past experience. I am probably just as biased as the next guy. Here is my two cents on the matter. I personally like replaceable blade fixed heads. If they are well designed I feel they are adequate in strength for any big game animal on the planet. Even if they are not as strong as non-replaceable fixed blade heads I feel the convenience of always having a razor sharp cutting edge far outweighs the slight disadvantage in strength. I have used many types of expanding heads as well over the years and while they do fly very well; I don't particularly like using them for species bigger than deer. I know they are generally strong enough to cleanly harvest game much larger, but I personally just like the strength of a fixed head. If maximum penetration is a concern, two factors come into play. Heavy arrows and cut-on-contact fixed blade heads are two features that will do more to improve penetration than all other factors combined.

ARCHERY ACCESSORIES

While all the accessories that go along with archery hunting are not a necessity, there are a few items that really will make a hunter much more successful. The first is a release. A quality release will help significantly with accuracy. Second is a good sight. Having a sight with easy-to-see pins (generally made out of fiber optic material) with smooth adjustments that stays set once sighted in is extremely important. After these two critical items I suggest purchasing a laser range finder. There are several models suitable for bow hunting that are small enough to slip into a shirt pocket. Most of these models are fast to use as well as extremely accurate. I personally have been using the Leupold RXII TBR (True Ballistic Range). This unit not only gives the linear range, but also simultaneously projects the true range when taking angles into consideration. This feature is ideal for the mountain hunter who is often confronted with estimating steep up or down shot angles.

I would guess that bow hunters miss the vast majority of shots today by misjudging the range; with a rangefinder you can control this variable to the best of your ability. There are many other accessories bow hunters will find themselves acquiring, and most of them work very well and are so individual in nature it is hard to suggest a right or wrong choice, it really just depends upon your own personal likes and dislikes. For example, I always use a bow-mounted quiver. I find it easier to use than a back or side quiver. I always know where my arrows are and don't think it unduly affects the balance of my bow, but I know several much more successful archers than I who

Getting and using a good quality rangefinder will go along way towards helping all hunters be more proficient shots on game.

despise bow mounted quivers and always opt to carry their arrows separately in a back mounted quiver. To each his own. This is the case with most archery accessories. From slings to dampening systems to rests, every hunter has his personal likes and dislikes and only time in the field will help you make up your mind about what works for your style of hunting.

MUZZLELOADERS

Next to bow hunting, muzzleloader hunters generally receive the next best big game seasons and can often get tags easier than modern rifle hunters. If you haven't tried muzzleloader hunting, there is no better time than the present. Muzzleloader hunting is really not as difficult as many would have you believe. Yes, it has its limitations in range and numbers of shots being available. When looked at in a practical manner, it is really not that big of a disadvantage. Most hunters with a bit of practice can effectively shoot a muzzleloader out to about 100 yards, and with a lot of practice and load development, I would argue that a muzzleloader can be an ethical 150-200 yard rifle in the right hands. Getting within 100 yards of most animals should be a doable proposition. In Western states I have shot elk, antelope, whitetails, and mule deer all with open sighted muzzleloaders. All of these animals are thought of as "long range" species, but with a little sneaking many hunters are able to get within 100 yards of each.

The first question most prospective front stuffers have is: what type of muzzleloader should I get; a traditional style rifle, or an inline?

Both of these guns will work fine on all North American big game and perform equally well. The choice between traditional or modern really is one of personal preference.

While traditional muzzleloaders will perform similar to a modern inline, the biggest difference boils down to ease of cleaning. No other muzzleloader is quite as easy to clean as the TC Triumph with its hand removable breech plug.

To many, inlines seem more like a modern rifle, seem much more effective and therefore some suggest not as challenging. I would argue that for the most part these assumptions are not true. I have hunted various big game species with both an inline muzzleloader as well as a traditional sidelock Hawkins rifle and for all practical purposes they are not that different. Yes, modern inlines appear to be more like a modern rifle but this is only skin deep, after the looks there aren't too many similarities. In all actuality both gun types will perform nearly identical and in some cases the traditional rifle may outperform the more "modern" inline. Both guns can be had in the same caliber, and if the right rate of twist is in the barrel, they will fire the exact same bullets to the same degree of accuracy. A longer barrel, (something a traditional gun generally has over a modern inline) actually will produce high velocities for the same load and the longer sight radius (distance between front and rear sight) makes using open sights more accurate. When it is all said and done the factors that contribute to the physical job of killing game: bullet size, weight, velocity and trajectory are identical between the two types of rifle.

Where an inline rifle shines is not in terms of performance, but in maintenance. The biggest challenge with any muzzleloader is unloading them and cleaning them on a regular basis. While the need to do this has decreased with some of the modern black

Most hunters today choose to use modern centerfire rifles for their big game hunting. Reliability, accuracy and easy of use makes up for the often hard to get tags and sometimes crowded hunting conditions.

powder substitutes it still has to be done frequently if you want to ward off rust and corrosion as well as keep the rifle reliable during a hunt. With a traditional muzzleloader this is quite an ordeal, which involves either firing the gun to remove the powder and bullet, using a pneumatic bullet remover or pulling the bullet with a rod. After the bullet and charge is removed traditional barreled guns need to be removed from the stock, and flushed out through the nipple hole with a bucket of hot soapy water.

With an inline all one has to do it remove the breech plug, push the bullet and charge all the way through and swab the barrel with oily patches from the rear much like a modern rifle with brushes and patches.

Next to maintenance the only other advantage an inline has to offers is a slight bit of edge in the reliability department in severely inclement weather. Since the breech end is generally covered, rain and snow have less of a chance of contaminating the cap and powder. In addition, the straight line of the cap spark to the powder charge reduces the chance of the flash not reaching the charge.

When it comes to selecting a caliber for all around big game hunting I generally choose either a .50 or .54. With the right bullets, not balls, either of these calibers will cleanly harvest all species of North American big game.

When making a decision on buying a muzzleloader, be sure to thoroughly read the rules and regulations on all states where you may be hunting. Several states have different (some of which are very strange) rules on what constitutes a legal muzzleloader. Some rules are based on action type, others on cap style, others on bullet size and weight in proportion to the bore diameter and there may be rules on sights. Be sure you thoroughly read all the regulations before heading afield.

As you can see there really are more similarities between an inline and a traditional muzzleloader than there are differences. They both still load from the front, they can only fire one load at a time and both need to use blackpowder or blackpowder substitutes. So get what appeals to you and what conforms to the states you plan on hunting and have fun.

MODERN RIFLE

The vast majority of hunters still head to the field with a modern centerfire rifle each year. Since its inception over 125 years ago, modern rifles have kept improving in reliability, accuracy, range and power. For big game hunting selecting the right rifle can be very critical. The decision should be based on the terrain you intend to hunt, the anticipated distance of the shot and the size of the game sought. Due to the terrain and anticipated distance of the shot of most western species choosing a rifle capable of stretching the range and increasing opportunities is a good idea. Luckily for hunters today there are many rifles that meet the minimum accuracy threshold for relatively long-range western big game hunting. Bolt actions typically dominate the accuracy scene, but good quality semi-autos, single shots, and pumps may also suffice. When it comes to selecting a caliber there are two schools of thought; get one caliber that works ok for everything or get a couple of rifles to cover the spectrum of big game species more precisely.

The advantages and disadvantages of each method are obvious. With a caliber that does it all, hunters have the advantage of being intimately familiar with their rifle's characteristics, point of aim, drop, trigger pull and feel. However the caliber is ideal in a relatively small window. It will probably be too large for some species such as antelope and possibly too small for species like moose.

For hunters looking to use one gun for all North American species, many feel the best all around choice is one of the various .30 calibers such as .30-06 Springfield, .308 Winchester, .300 Winchester mag, or .300 WSM. The advantages of the various .30 calibers are the wide range of bullet weights available, ammo availability around the world, and manageable recoil combined with enough energy

Recently introduced, the Thompson Center Icon is a great looking, good shooting, bolt action rifle that sports styling traits of both classic American design and old world European influence. Features includes, changeable bolt handle, integral scope mounts, and a detachable single stack magazine.

Premium ammo like the Federal line works wonderfully on a wide spectrum of game. When going on a dream hunt, don't leave anything to chance and use the best premium ammo that shoots well in your particular firearm.

to handle most game species. While either end of the bullet weight spectrum covers more territory than most hunters will choose (.30 caliber bullets can be had in lightweight 55 grain sabots designed for varmints up to 220 grain round nose bullets), from a practical standpoint, there are some incredibly well-constructed 150 to 165 grain bullets that are fast and flat shooting making them idea for antelope and long range deer hunting applications, while the bonded 180 grain bullets can work great for elk, bear and even moose, making anything heavier not necessary.

The advantages of having one rifle not withstanding, for hunters who like to own more than one big game rifle and desire a perfect caliber for small, medium and large big game species a three gun combo may be more apropos. Smaller species such as southern whitetail, javelina and antelope don't require much more than any of the various .25 calibers (or less) provide. Calibers such as .243 WSM, .243 Winchester, .25 WSM, .25-06 all work perfectly for these smaller critters. When it comes to mid-sized game such as sheep, mule deer, and caribou look at the mid-sized calibers. Anything from a .270 Winchester through a .300 Winchester Magnum will work fine. Some very popular favorites include: .270 WSM, .270 Winchester, 7mm Remington Magnum, .308 Winchester, .30-06, .300 WSM, and .300

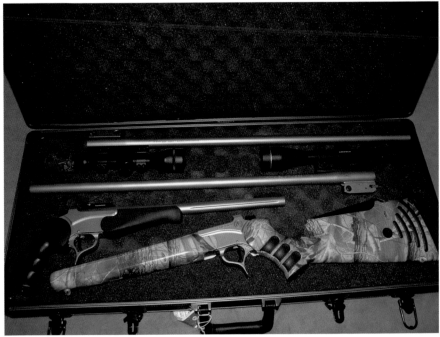

The TC Encore really is the best of all worlds. Not only is it incredibly accurate, it can quickly be converted from a handgun to a rifle, to a muzzleloader to a shotgun in virtually any caliber.

Winchester Magnum. Finally for the largest big game species North America offers (large southeast Alaska black bears, brown bears, moose and bison), calibers in the 325 WSM, .338 Winchester Magnum, 338 Federal and even the .375 H&H are all excellent choices.

THE BEST OF BOTH WORLDS – THE TC ENCORE PRO HUNTER

It is an often debated topic – should a hunter have multiple rifles/calibers for different species such as antelope, whitetails and elk or should he have one rifle that he knows inside and out, can shoot with confidence and will work, if not ideal for a spectrum of game. Thomson Center possibly has the best solution in their extremely popular Encore Pro Hunter. The Pro Hunter is an evolution of their standard Encore, a beefed up and slightly improved version of their original single shot Contender.

What makes this platform so popular among hunters is that it is essentially one firearm that with a quick swap out of a barrel (can be converted in less than 5 minutes with just a screwdriver) can be made to work for any application. The important criteria such as stock fit, weight, balance and trigger pull all remain the same, just the caliber changes From .22 LR to a .50 caliber muzzleloader, to any one of hundreds of different centerfire rifle calibers to even a shotgun barrel – this one platform can literally be customized to be perfect for squirrels or elephant or anything in between. In addition to the myriad of rifle barrels available for the Encore, it is also an ideal platform for hunters looking for an excellent long-range handgun. By replacing the butt stock with a pistol grip, swapping out the forends and adding a short pistol barrel hunters instantly have a tack driving long-range handgun capable of tackling anything in North America.

HANDGUN

Handgun hunting is increasing in popularity across the nation. Many hunters are gravitating to the pure challenge of it, some like their weight; others just simply like the handiness of not lugging a rifle around. For whatever reason handgun hunting is growing by leaps and bounds. Unlike bow or muzzleloader hunting where

The Encore handgun can be chambered for many calibers large enough to cover any big game in the world. In addition to power, it is incredibly accurate producing groups on par with many rifles.

there is a seasonal advantage for choosing one of these tools, for the most part there are very few special seasons for handgun hunters. If a person hunts with a handgun it usually falls within the modern rifle season. For this reason most handgun hunters are doing so just for the pure challenge of it or for weight reduction. Some states have shotgun zones where centerfire rifles are not legal for use. In these zones, muzzleloaders are legal, and in some states such as Wisconsin, handguns are legal in these areas too. All of this adds to the growing popularity of handgun hunting.

Modern day handgun hunters have several choices of handguns to choose from, but the most common are either single shots designed with hunting in mind such as the TC Encore, Contender or G2, or a large caliber revolver.

Of all the single shots the most common is the Thompson Center. Back in 1967 the first single shot that rolled off their production line was the venerable Contender. A modern marvel of power in its day, the Contender has lauded for incredible accuracy, excellent workmanship and the ability to fire a whole host of calibers that were never before thought suitable for a handgun. While the Contender was very diverse, it was only designed to handle low-pressure cartridges. Thompson Center has recently redesigned the Contender, called the G2 and Encore, and made some subtle changes in internal workings, but most importantly beefed up the action to handle high-pressure cartridges. This opened the door to hunting cartridges such as the 7mm-08, 270 Winchester and 30-06, making the Encore a true multi-species big game handgun right off the shelf. Available with or without iron sights the Encore makes a tremendous hunting handgun for a variety of big game species.

In revolvers there are many more choices than in single shot handguns. Smith and Wesson, Ruger, Colt, Freedom Arms, Magnum Research and several custom gunsmiths such as Linebaugh, and Gary Reeder make excellent hunting handguns. For those that thought the biggest revolver cartridge was a .44 magnum, they need to think again. In recent years not only the bore diameter, but also the power level of handgun hunting cartridges has been ratcheting up producing cartridges on energy par with many low-pressure centerfire rifle cartridges. The .44 Remington Magnum is now just the starting platform for serious revolver hunters, cartridges such as the .480 Ruger, .454 Casull, .475 Linnebaugh, .460 Smith and Wesson. .45-70 and the largest of them all the .500 Smith and Wesson are now readily available in several production handguns.

CROSSBOWS

The number of hunters choosing to pick up a crossbow for big game in America is increasing at an extremely fast pace – and for good reason. Traditionally thought of as only a viable tool for physically challenged folks, more and more hunters are seeing them for what they really are; accurate, efficient and just plain fun! If you needed a reason, crossbows are ideal for younger hunters, and for some women who struggle with drawing a bow as well as with older bow hunters who no longer can pull a traditional vertical bow.

Crossbows are cocked either with both hands and your back or many have a built in cocking devise that can literally be operated by the meekest person. Most crossbows today are fitted with a scope, and are pretty darn accurate. Taking up crossbow shooting for the first time, I chose to hunt with a Tenpoint Phantom. It is an excellent machine that launches bolts well over 320fps and even in my shaking hands is plenty accurate out to 60 yards. Using their built in monopod

Hunting with a crossbow is a great challenge for all hunters regardless of physical condition. It combines the skill needed to be a successful bowhunter with the familiar hold of a rifle so many hunters are accustomed to.

Crossbows have come along way in the last 20 years. Today they are extremely accurate and powerful. Many states are now realizing they are not just for physically challenged hunters, but suitable for all hunters looking for another mode to harvest game.

style rest from the sitting position I was able to keep all five shot within a 5 inch diameter circle at 60 yards. These new generations of crossbows really are shooting machines.

Every state has different regulations concerning the use of crossbows, and they are changing every season. Be sure to check the regulation web site listed in the resource guide section of this book for updated state-by-state information.

OUTFITTER GRADE OPTICS

I have said this before and I will say it again, optics are equally important as a rifle, bow, muzzleloader or handgun – in fact I consider them more important in some cases. This is especially true when hunting the open country of the West. Every year I hunt whitetails in the Midwest with a set of compact binoculars in my pack more out of habit than necessity. For most hardwoods, whitetail hunts you simply don't need them. However, out west for elk, mule deer or sheep you will quickly realize that without quality optics you are at a serious disadvantage. When going on a guided hunt, having good optics (especially a high end spotting scope) is part of a good guide's responsibility. When you go after big game on your own, that responsibility becomes yours. In order to have the success rate of an outfitter, you need to have outfitter grade optics.

Start by choosing binoculars, they are the most used piece of optics a western hunter will own. In my book they must have several key features to make the grade. To begin with the glass has to be first rate. This means fully multi-coated, high quality and exceptionally clear lenses with good definition between light and dark regions. Clarity should extend from edge to edge, not just at a spot in the center. Try reading the smallest print on a sign a distance away while scanning from edge to edge, poor quality glass will prove itself inferior rather quick. After that, the optics need to be fog and moisture proof, have good light transmitting capabilities and be in a power I prefer to use all day, (this typically is around 8-power). I like this power for big game hunting, as the models are generally a bit lighter and easier to pack than comparable 10-power models. Being of a lesser power the field of view is larger allowing you to scan more real estate. In addition, the 8-power models are easy to hold, and reduce eyestrain.

Out West, having good optics can make or break a hunt. Many days are spent behind them looking for game, so buy the best you can afford and use them often.

For field judging trophies, nothing compares to a good spotting scope. A quality spotting scope can save miles on your feet, not to mention lots of time.

On higher-powered models, the "shake" becomes more apparent and really there is not enough increase in power to truly field judge trophy animals. That is what spotting scopes are for.

Most eastern hunters do not use spotting scopes very much, if at all. Out West, however, they are as common as a spare tire in the bed of a pickup. Most ranchers, guides and hunters always have one handy. And for judging trophy potential, nothing beats a good spotting scope. It could save your feet miles of agony in checking out animals that ultimately you don't want to shoot, or it can light up your mood when you see "Mr. Wallhanger." Most good quality spotting scopes have variable power that zoom within a given range. Very typically this range is 20-60 power. This is a nice feature as on 20 power you can still scan a hillside looking for bedded game and once found, you can zoom in to 45-60 power for a very detailed look at their antlers. Unlike binoculars, spotting scopes have to be rested or supported in some fashion to be used effectively. In its simplest form "rested" means across a pack or a rolled up jacket laid across a downed tree. While these basic supports work, a high quality adjustable tripod is much better. For a backpack hunt, small lightweight tabletop sized tripods work fine, but if you will be using the spotting scope a lot, a full sized tripod with a good quality swiveling photographic-style head works the best because it can be adjusted to any height or at any angle for comfortable long hours of glassing. It is also a good idea to have a window mount. These mounts affix to the spotting scope then clamp on a half open vehicle window. During pre-season scouting from roads, nothing beats this set up for ease of use and comfort.

The final optical component that hunters need to review is the riflescope. Like other optical devices it pays to buy the best you can afford. After all the money and time is spent preparing for a big game hunt, traveling to the location, waiting years for the right tag and purchasing all the ancillary gear needed to finally get a shot, a cheap scope that has shifted point of impact or has fogged up is not a great investment. Riflescopes really are no different than binoculars or spotting scopes. Hunters need to have fully multi-coated optics, that are fog and rain proof and built rugged enough to withstand the rigors of the outdoors. Like other forms of optics I classify riflescopes in three rough categories: premium, middle-of-the-road and poor. The top two tiers are all you want to look at as a serious hunter. Avoid the lower tier optics. You will not be happy with them and eventually will replace them with the optics you should have bought in the first place.

Quality binoculars will be water and fog proof, shock resistant and have high quality glass that transmits light well, separates dark from light areas and remains clear from edge to edge.

When buying optics, you get what you pay for. Unlike clothing, packs, or even rifles (where a $300 bargain basement gun can shoot as well as a $5,000 engraved high-end rifle), this does not happen in optics. There really are no unfound bargains that perform on par with the best for a fraction of the price.

I worked several years for a large outdoor retailer and as part of a program to educate employees, all of the optics they carried (which was essentially all in the world) were made available for up to a two-month check out for use in the field. This gave employees the in-the-field knowledge and experience with optics that they could probably not afford and a breadth of experience with all optics that very few people get to experience regardless of wealth. Over the course of several years I think I used every major brand of optics, both binocular and spotting scope under a variety of conditions. What I found shouldn't shock anyone. The most expensive pieces of glass outperformed the cheaper models – hands down. If you haven't had the opportunity to use a set of Swarovskis, Zeiss, Kahles or the high-end Nikon Premier or Leupold line in the field, you don't know what you are missing. Everything else pales in comparison. If you can afford it, getting the right optics is simple, go out and buy any of the above listed brands in a configuration that suits your hunting needs and style and you will be happy. However, the problems arise when you can't afford to spend well over the thousand dollar mark to look at game and trust me I am in the same boat. What options are left? Luckily there are many. The next tier down is what I call the middle-of-the-road optics. This is generally comprised of standard Leupold and Nikon, some upper-end Bushnell, some house brands, and Steiner. In this category there are some real sleeper units that will perform almost on par with the lower end of the premium units at a fraction of the price. A hunter looking at buying the upper end of these middle priced units can expect to spend less than half of most premium prices optics and will get 85-90% of the quality. It is that last 10% that the premium units offer that costs exponentially more.

Below the middle-priced units, simply put, I wouldn't waste my money. Bargain priced optics are generally junk that will invariably be replaced down the road with what should have been bought the first time around. If bargain priced optics are all you can afford, I suggest not buying any at all. Look for used, or borrow from a friend, until you can purchase the model you want that will last many years, if not a lifetime.

CHAPTER 5

Your Home In The Wilderness

I t was 4:30 am and the alarm was buzzing in my ear. I slowly sat up in the tent and groped for my headlamp. My breath hung suspended in frozen clouds in its beam. Getting out of that warm mummy bag was the last thing I wanted to do, but I knew in two short hours I would be sitting on a ridge watching herds of elk funnel through the valley – no matter how cold the morning, it was a sight not to be missed.

No one can tell me that all fall camping is fun. It can be a lot of work, it can be extremely cold, it can be wet and it often requires a substantial amount of gear to remain comfortable. But for public land hunters looking to access remote country or hunters trying to optimize a budget it may be the best way.

Accessing Backcountry

As I have said before, one of the biggest nemeses of public land hunts is the "public." If the tag was easily obtained, chances are you will not be alone come opening day. However, I have witnessed time and time again a reluctance of most hunters to travel very far from a vehicle access point. Generally "very far" means about two miles. When it comes to very steep, mountainous country cut that distance in half.

By setting up a base camp deep in the wilderness several miles from any vehicle access you immediately get past 90% of the other hunters and have a much shorter hike to the prime hunting area each morning.

Accessing this base camp may be obtained in several ways (horseback, ATV, light airplane, mountain bike or on foot) depending upon where you are hunting. Let's focus on the most common, and least expensive; your own two feet.

The author heading afield in Alaska in Dehavilland Beaver. Type of hunt tests the limits of lightweight hunting.

When hunting on foot, every item must be packed on your back so only bring the bare essentials needed for your stay. Ounces quickly turn into pounds the further one gets from a trailhead. A strong adult can comfortably carry a 60-75 pound pack for several miles if the pack is well constructed and distributes the weight to the shoulders and waist. If you can't keep the gear needed to less than 75 pounds you need to start pairing down your gear. The itemized list below will help prospective back country hunters select the right gear, but still remain comfortable.

BASIC BACK COUNTRY PACKING LIST

Packs

Packs traditionally have been of two styles; soft sided, quiet and often small hunting or "day" packs and larger bulky pack frames.

I prefer day packs that are quiet, water resistant (few are waterproof) and have lots of small pockets. Ideally you will have a separate spot for your knife, flashlight, medical kit, emergency food, extra ammo and spotting scope. Nothing is worse than having only one compartment where all this equipment bangs together, makes noise and ultimately get scratched and worn out prematurely.

Pack frames are also a necessity for the backcountry hunter. They provide the support needed for carrying large bulky items in and out of the field. While many hikers use internal frame packs, for a hunter who may likely be carrying large bulky quarters of meat out of the woods, I still prefer an external metal frame. Pack frames come in many different levels of quality and like most things in life you get what you pay for. Inexpensive units are not comfortable, they rattle and squeak and ultimately may fail when you need them most.

Carrying a load

For hunters looking to carry a serious load as well as pack out quarters of meat the available packs that will fill this bill well diminish rapidly. Two that stand out are the Kirafu series and the Mystery Ranch series by Dana Design. Kifaru makes several models of packs ranging from their small day stalker to their massive 8,500 cubic inch Rendezvous Long Hunter that can also be separated from the duplex frame to serve double duty as an excellent freighter frame. Additional features include: removable camo panels that reverse to blaze orange, gun bearer cradle, and multiple compression straps.

The Mystery Ranch packs are also another great design for hunters on the move. Built to withstand anything Mother Nature or careless users can throw at them, they are nearly bomb-proof. Their NICE frame system is extremely well designed to handle heavy loads of game meat or can be used in conjunction with their various bags and packs to create a custom gear hauling pack.

Both of these packs are completely compressible when used with smaller loads, and can be cinched down to serve as a day pack or expanded to whatever size is needed.

Quality units are generally lighter weight, solidly welded and squeak-proof and have a very comfortable padded harness system that makes carrying large loads much more comfortable.

However, the down side to pack frames comes on your daily hunt. If you knew you were going to shoot an animal that particular day, planning for the day and consequently what pack to bring afield would be an easy task, but that is never the case. Most days are single day hikes away from camp where a small pack will suffice, but some days the weather may get bad, you may get stranded in a remote stretch of woods after dark and want to spend the night or you may actually down an animal and wish you had a frame to pack part of him back to camp. Until recently there has not been a good solution for the wilderness hunter combining the best of both the day pack and the pack frame.

I have used my day pack strapped to a pack frame bringing them both afield at the same time. This works relatively well, but not perfectly. More recently however a newer generation of packs specifically designed to solve this two pack dilemma has emerged. Offered by several manufacturers (see side bar on packs) these packs

A quality pack like this Long Hunter from Kifaru is ideal for extended stays in the wilderness as well as for hauling large bulky loads like quarters of game back out of the field.

are essentially the best of both worlds. They have the pockets and bags necessary to serve as a day pack, but are attached to a heavy duty freighter-style frame. The packs can be expanded very large or snugged down to be small and close fitting when used as a day pack. If an animal is taken they can be expanded to accept a quarter, cape, skull, etc and serve as a freighter. While nothing is perfect, the packs described in the side bar are as close as I have found for wilderness adventurers planning to carry their home on their back and stay for an extended time.

Tents

Selecting the right tent for your backcountry excursion really depends upon how many people are going, what type of weather is anticipated and how far into the backcountry you plan on traveling. Plan for the worst possible scenario and you

The Super Tarp by Kifaru is an excellent option for hunters looking for the ultimate in weight savings and packability. It is also the only tent in its class that can accept a wood burning stove. This tent, when combined with their ultralight wood burning stove, still weighs significantly less than many other comparable shelters without a stove.

will be fine. Make sure that all tents are designed for four season use even if you don't anticipate using them in the middle of winter. Having the extra protection and quality will pay dividends should a freak fall storm roll in.

As a general rule of thumb, unless you are trying to save every ounce of weight, double the size of the tent for the number of people. If you are going solo, get a two person tent; for you and a partner get a four person tent and so on. The extra space will provide enough room to store gear and spread out a bit and ultimately doesn't weigh that much more.

If you are truly trying to cut every ounce of weight look at some creative options such as the product line from Kifaru. This is a company that knows what it is like to pack everything in on one's back. The owner and founder Patrick Smith while in his 60's still spends over 150 nights under the stars field testing and developing products. Their line of single walled tipis and advanced tarps are really all anyone can ask for in a lightweight offering. Made from material that is extremely lightweight, but very tough these shelters are designed with function in mind. The nice thing about their product line (including their Para Tipi and Para Tarp) is that most of their shelters can accept their ultra light collapsible backpacking wood stove. At under three pounds this stove can work wonders at warming up the tent and drying out gear.

Sleeping bag

Luckily for today's hunters sleeping bags are light years ahead of where they were just a generation ago. They are lighter, warmer and more compact than ever before. But selecting the right sleeping bag to suit your backcountry needs, really depends on several factors. For the ultimate in lightweight and compactness it is hard to beat traditional down filled bags, however if the hunt is going to be wet and there is not an opportunity to dry the bag, within a few days body moisture will collect in the bag and reduce the loft and insulating properties making it nearly worthless. For this reason on wet hunts, synthetic fill material is a better choice. Choose a bag that is made for serious backcountry use and rated below (in terms of temperature) the anticipated temperature on your hunt. Mummy style bags offer the best warmth to weight ratio and stuff into a smaller space due to their cut, but if you don't like the restrictiveness of a mummy bag, semi-mummy and square bags will work fine as well – they will just weigh a bit more and take up slightly more space. Whatever style and material you choose make sure your bag

Having a quality light is necessary for the backcountry hunter. The author carries several including a Sure-Fire flashlight and a Cyclops headlamp/hat bill lamp.

has layered insulation to eliminate cold spots, zipper baffles (to keep cold air from transferring through the zipper) and some sort of draw string/hood system to keep body and head heat inside the bag.

Sleeping pad

Next to a sleeping bag the most important piece of equipment for a comfortable night's sleep is a sleeping pad. Sleeping pads come in several forms but their primary function remains the same. They all need to provide cushion from the hard ground, a moisture barrier from damp conditions and insulation from the cold. Sleeping pads come in many thicknesses and weights from the ultralight to nearly a standard household mattress, but hunter's carrying their gear in on their own two feet should look at the most compact and lightest offerings. Closed cell foam as well as "self-inflating" models work great and can be rolled up tight and strapped securely to a pack. If you are using a self inflating model like the Therma Rest which I personally prefer, be sure to pack a small patch kit in case the pad gets punctured from a sharp rock or stick.

Flashlights and Headlamps

Look for several key features when selecting a good flashlight or headlamp - a rugged body, waterproof construction, bright bulb (along with built in space for a spare) and quality construction throughout. When hunting the backcountry pack both a flashlight and a headlamp as they both come in handy for different jobs and should one break you will have a spare. I use a compact Surefire flashlight for much of the activities around camp. But I like the dual dexterity I get from a quality headlamp or even a hat brim mounted Cyclops when doing chores or skinning out an animal after dark.

There is no need to carry extra weight into the back country to prepare meals. Today hunters can choose from several makers of ultra-lightweight stoves and lanterns as well as titanium cookware.

Ultra light Cooking and Camp Equipment

Since every ounce counts when you are hiking in mountainous country take a look at upgrading standard aluminum or steel nestling camp cookware for much lighter titanium units. Titanium (Ti) is incredibly light and strong making it an ideal choice for backcountry camping. Pots, pans, cups and silverware are available in Ti. Replace a few of the larger items and see if it doesn't lighten you load. Also cups and plates made from high impact plastic are lightweight and don't burn your lips or chill your food because the conduct less heat than metal.

Like Ti cookware, lightweight single burner stoves are all about saving weight - 10 miles from the truck on the side of the mountain is no place to pack in a traditional multi burner stove. Available in several varieties from white gas to multi-fuel to butane fired, there are more single burner stoves on the market today than ever before. There are even super-light models made from Ti that weight only a couple of ounces.

A lightweight single element lantern to use in the backcountry can help cut size and weight. Several companies including Brunton and Snow Peak are making excellent Pietzo ignition ultralight single element lanterns that are well worth the look and Brunton's new line of practically indestructible mantle-less lanterns are ideal. I like having a lantern in camp and if I can fit it in, always bring one. But if you must shave every ounce this item can be left behind since you can get by with a flashlight and headlamp.

Water purification methods

When backcountry camping (in most places in the world) it is not a good idea to drink straight from a natural water source such as a lake or river (springs may be safe, but still questionable) so precautions must be taken. There are several ways of purifying your water including boiling, chemicals and commercial purification units. A hard rolling boil for 5 minutes will make any water safe to drink, but it does involve some prep time and equipment and it leaves the water very flat tasting. Chemical purification in the form of tablets or liquid is another very safe option, but some kind of flavor such powdered juice mix will have to be added to cover the slight chemical taste. Far and away my favorite method is the mechanical backpacker-style water purification unit. These come in many sizes, have different levels of protection and in general are very fast, lightweight and easy to use. They also provide a more palatable result.

Emergency First Aid Kit

This portion of your gear is an absolute necessity and should never be left outside of the pack. In my big game fanny pack, which I have with me at all times in the field I carry a relatively compact first aid kit that is capable of taking care of most emergencies encountered. A basic emergency first aid kit can be purchased preassembled or can

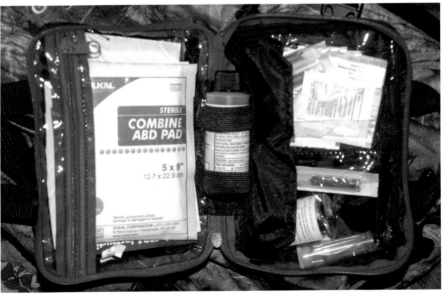

No matter if you are just hiking a few hundred yards from camp or heading out on an extended wilderness trip, be sure to pack a complete first aid kit to deal with minor discomforts as well as major medical issues.

be bought a la carte. The basic items should include: all prescribed medications, bandages, Band-Aids, laxatives, anti-diarrhea, antacid, aspirin, anti- allergy/sinus, a section of rubber surgical tubing to be used as a tourniquet, sling material, butterfly closure bandages (only have sutures/surgical staples if you are trained in their use), burn ointment, antiseptic such as iodine or hydrogen peroxide, and Neosporin. The key for a backcountry hunter is to have everything you may need, but not so much that it unduly weighs the pack down. Look for ways to be complete, but still cut weight. As an example, I feel hydrogen peroxide is a necessity, but I don't need a full 9 ounce bottle on a trip. I buy small, high-quality screw top plastic 1 ounce bottles and fill them with the various liquids. Mark the outside of the bottle with permanent pen with their contents and you are fully prepared with much less weight. That way all the supplies needed can be taken and the average person can still lift the pack off the ground.

When it comes to backcountry hunting there are many small items that need to be included in a pack. Everyone is different and needs vary by the person, but here is a sample of some of the miscellaneous items I keep in my pack.

GPS

GPS units are a must have item in every pack. I mention them in the survival section of this book, but outside of survival they are in incredible hunting tool. Pocket sized and lightweight, they can mark a deer rub line, an elk wallow or camp making finding any of the above, even in the dark as simple as following an arrow. With the ease of use, affordability and portability there is no reason every hunter shouldn't have a GPS

Water bottle

A water bottle comes in very handy for purifying water, making soup or carrying water afield. Most packs today have a side pouch designed for their storage. Be sure to buy a quality water bottle from companies like Nalgeen as they are food-grade safe and have a lids that will not leak. Also many of the attachments such as coffee filters and water purification units are specifically designed to fit this type of bottle.

Multi tool

A multi tool such as the Gerber Diesel can be worth its weight in gold on a backcountry hunt. From opening cans to fixing broken equipment the number of tasks they can do seems never ending.

Having a good selection of cutting tools including a knife, saw and multi tool not only make game processing, but camping much easier.

Windproof Lighter

I keep a store of matches and fire starting equipment buried in my survival kit. I also always try to keep a high-quality Brunton butane, windproof lighter handy in a side pocket of my pack. A quality lighter is perfect for lighting stoves and starting fires with damp material.

Repair Kit

In my pack I keep a small repair kit that covers almost any problems I may encounter while afield. The kit includes some extra webbing straps, extra buckles for the pack, boot laces, a nearly empty roll of duct tape smashed flat, glue and seam sealer for the tent and patching material for waterproof items. While it never is fully complete, by anticipating things that may break and keeping spares you can eliminate a lot of the worry from backcountry travel.

AVOIDING CAMP PROBLEMS

Depending upon where you are hunting, large carnivores such as bears may or may not be a serious threat. Large carnivores are increasing their range across the United States and if it is truly big

Two Wheel Camping

Depending upon the terrain, hunters may have a better way to access the backcountry than on foot alone. Most backcountry areas across the United States do not allow motorized vehicles of any kind, but many do allow horses as well as pedal powered mountain bikes.

Horses require a large investment and a year around commitment far beyond what most hunters want to provide, but a mountain bike on the other hand is relatively affordable, easily maintained and doesn't eat thousands of pounds of hay. If the country has good trails or even old, out-of-service logging roads you can easily cut the time down to a quarter of what it takes to hike in. Even if it is so rugged that riding is out of the question, a mountain bike makes a great off road "wheelbarrow" to transport gear into the field.

Mountain bikes can be equipped with bow/gun racks, side panniers, front and rear racks to pretty much carry all of the gear needed for an extended stay in the wilderness. In addition to getting all of the gear in when an animal is shot the quarters as well as the rack and cape, can be strapped to the bike and the bike wheeled out making the entire process much easier on your back than carrying it all out on a pack frame. Incidentally, always mark the cape and antlers with multiple strips of red surveyors tape when transporting game out of the field whether you are on a bike or on foot.

game country bears will be in the same general vicinity. That being said, avoiding run-ins with them is relatively easy to accomplish.

Don't cook inside or around a tent. The smell from cooking will linger in the area and may lure a bear into a camp to tear it up. Far better, cook at least 100 yards away from camp on the downwind side. Food storage is also critical. Hang all meat and food products well away from camp in a high tree or suspended between two trees even works better as black bears are notoriously good climbers. Quarters of meat can be placed in heavy duty canvas game bags and hung. If flies are not a problem they can be hung without any covering. The best way I have found to hang food is a length of parachute cord and a large nylon stuff sack. Keep all your food inside, close the top, tie it off with cord and hoist it into the tree. This will keep it relatively safe from bears, and all the other small animals such as pack rats, camp jays and mice that can be become a pest in the backcountry.

Lightweight RV Campers and Semi-Remote Hunting

I am not a huge fan of RV camping because most are limited to travel on pretty well-established roadways and use in modern campgrounds. There is a place under some conditions for small, lightweight off road trailers as well as truck bed campers. I have enjoyed several western hunts out of both of these rigs and the difference they make in your attitude and overall comfort level on a hunt is incredible. Obviously they can't be used for back country hunting, but can serve as a base camp or be used in areas that have less hunting pressure. Most modern campers are not only dry and warm, they have running water, stoves, refrigerator, a toilet, shower and room to store plenty of gear and hunting accessories. To sleep in a warm comfortable bed after a good meal cooked on a stove and keep the rest of your food cold or frozen means you can stay afield a lot longer, more comfortably than the guy simply camping out. Whether used as a full time camp or a base camp an RV camper can provide a welcome wilderness home.

Budget Minded Camping

Being that one of this book's main goals is hunting on a budget, I would be remiss if I didn't at least cover a bit of budget camping gear. I do not propose cutting corners on things that are important. Being frugal on relatively inexpensive camping items is possibly the worst decision hunters can make. The overall cost of a big game trip far

PREPARING FOR THE WORST

When you are camping far from civilization it is just smart to consider the worst possible scenario and take some precautions. With today's world of technology this is easier to do than ever before. Satellite phones can keep you connected literally anywhere in the world. I am not suggesting bringing one so you can keep in touch with the office, but it is nice to have one should something go seriously wrong and you need immediate help. Satellite phones are now relatively small and affordable. If you don't have one and are only taking one trip into the backcountry a year you may be better off to rent one instead of buying one. There are several companies that rent satellite phones for a very reasonable amount on a daily, weekly or monthly basis. They are all set up and ready to go with a standard per minute rate charged to your credit card when they are used.

exceeds the cost of having the right gear. The quality of that gear often means the difference from staying out in rough conditions or pulling stakes and going home (i.e. success or failure). But that being said, if your hunt is being squeezed right down to the financial bone here are some ways to save without sacrificing quality.

Choose house branded gear from a reputable retailer. This is comparable to buying store brand food products from a large chain store. The food is certainly of good quality and possibly grown and packed by the same processor as the national brand. Many of the big retailers such as Gander Mountain make their own branded merchandise. Most of the time this gear is designed on par if not superior to "name brand" similar merchandise and is generally offered at a lesser price. Everything from tents, to clothing to packs are available as a house brand and customers can generally expect to save 10-25%.

Instead of buying cheaper products across the board, look at cutting out non-essential items and using the saved money to buy the best in required items. Personally, I consider a tent, pack, sleeping bag and sleeping pad must have items and I want the best. I can do without: a water purification system (use tablets, which taste bad, but are cheap), lightweight stove (cook on an open fire), titanium pots and pans (use cheaper aluminum or eat only foods that come in a bag, can be cooked on a stick or do not require cooking at all such as MRE's, tuna, jerky, nuts, etc). My father did a do-it-yourself high alpine mountain goat hunt nearly 50 years ago and cooked all meals out of several different size coffee cans with wire bails which nestled inside of each other. I like a small lantern, but if I was seriously cutting costs could do without one, utilizing only a headlamp. Another great option for cutting costs is used gear. Garage sales, online sites and shops specializing in used camping gear can be a bargain hunter's dream come true. Keep your eyes open for a deal, pair down your list to essentials and you can outfit a camp for a fraction of what you thought possible.

Ultralight camping

Unlike bargain camping, ultralight camping is not about saving money, but size and weight. You will quickly find that the price goes up as the ounces go down, but for super remote backcountry applications or fly in trips where hunters are severely limited to the amount of gear allowed ultralight camping equipment is the only option.

I well remember the first time I chartered a Super Cub to take me into the backcountry of Alaska for a caribou hunt. When I initially heard I could bring in 50 pounds of gear plus my rifle I thought I would have plenty of weight to spare. I was much younger and more naïve then and hadn't really weighed my pack before. Packing for the trip at home I put my pack on the scale and was shocked to learn it was closer to 70 pounds than 50 and I hadn't yet put in a week's worth of food…I was in serious trouble.

This is the type of camping where every unnecessary item is left out and every necessary item is scrutinized, reviewed and re-bought in a lighter version if possible. When you are tying to cut serious weight start by looking at the pack itself. Depending upon the material, padding, internal support, straps and number of accessory pockets and zippers, it can weigh quite a bit. Don't get a pack based on weight, but once you have narrowed your choices down to several suitable packs do look at their comparable weights. Another big offender is the tent. For most hunts that require a lightweight tent you also want a very good quality four season tent (the backcountry in Alaska or the Rocky Mountains is not a place to have a three season tent because it is lightweight). Therein lies the problem. However,

I wondered after I took this photo, "Where am I going to sit?" Luckily another plane touched down to ferry me, and the rest of my hunting party, back to civilization. Having to rely on just those few pounds of gear you can bring in with you is the thrill and challenge of doing one of these hunts!

there are several small 1-3 man units that can withstand the rigors of backcountry weather and still come in under 5 pounds. Sleeping bags are the next weight problem. Again, you don't want to skimp on this part of your gear. Down is the lightest insulation material, but it does have the disadvantage of losing loft if it gets wet. They can be a great lightweight choice, but you must be careful to keep them dry and hopefully have the right weather to dry them out during the day from the previous night's body moisture. They can be had in the three pound range, which is adequate for most temperature ranges. If you are a dedicated minimalist another good sleeping bag option is the MOB from Kifaru. This sleeping bag is a synthetic filled model with a tough Rhino Skin shell that can be zipped apart in sections. The theory is that different sections can be used to meet different temperature ranges as well as the upper half serving as clothing during the day. By eliminating some of your clothing, this bag can help lighten your overall load.

When it comes to cooking equipment go with titanium everything. Serious backcountry campers have been using titanium stoves, bowls, cups and utensils for quite some time and although expensive, nothing beats the weight savings. You will quickly find that food

Hunters wishing to lighten their load as well as increase their hunting time should consider easy to prepare, lightweight foods such as instant freeze dried meals, jerky, nuts and protein bars. To help replace vitamins and minerals, or cover the taste of purified water, lightweight powders like Propel work well.

weighs a lot, but it falls within the "very necessary" category. Look at bringing freeze dried food, high protein bars, jerky, and protein powder. For carbohydrates pancake mix, packets of noodles, Top Ramon, mac and cheese and spaghetti with dried cheese like mazithra. You always hope you can supplement this diet with fresh backstraps, wild berries and possibly trout, but don't count on it. Go prepared with enough food to last the duration with a comfortable buffer in case you get lost, stranded or the plane is late.

WHAT'S FOR DINNER?

When hiking and hunting all day, you can't hardly put on weight – in fact without consuming foods high in calories, you will probably go home a few pounds lighter. But what foods should you be eating while on a back country hunting trip? Well balanced for sure, high in energy and easy to consume are often the main criteria, but depending on how you traveled to the wilderness will mainly be the determining factor on exactly what you eat.

If you are hiking or flying into an area, forget about bringing heavy, water-soaked objects such as potatoes, fresh meats and produce – especially if you are staying for any length of time – you just can't afford the weight. Instant or near instant food are the way to go. There are several companies today making excellent backpacker-style freeze dried food just for this purpose and they work terrific. These freeze dried meals are available in literally dozens of "flavors" for lunch, dinner and breakfast. They weigh mere ounces apiece and are packed with enough calories to satisfy a growling stomach. In addition to being lightweight they are just plain convenient. When going on a trophy big game hunt, you want to maximize your time in the field hunting, not preparing culinary delights and doing dishes. For this reason many hunters, even those with weight and space to spare (horseback or RV bound) choose instant meals while afield – they are just plain quick and simple to prepare, with no mess afterwards. Not a lot of cooking utensils need to be packed either. A medium sized aluminum or titanium cup capable of holding 16 ounces of water, a single burner backpacker stove and a spork are all that are really needed for a week's trip. Boil the water, pour it right into the instant meal's bag, close up and let soak and eat right from the bag. Wash out the contents of the bag and the spork and dishes are done. The entire meal process can be done while perched on a mountainside glassing for game.

In addition to convenience, another reason freeze dried food work so well – they require no refrigeration and last for many years in their original package. Remote hunters don't have the option of keeping perishable items cool all the time, a cooler with ice is not a viable option.

To spice up the diet a bit as well as provide some instant energy without setting up a stove, be sure to pack a large variety of energy bars. These are easily consumed, come in many flavors and the good news is they now taste much better than ever. I personally prefer several of the varieties of Wilderness Athlete bars. Also pack along a good selection of granola bars to help round out the diet.

Trail mix is another good option for food on the go. Its weight-to-energy ratio is good and can be easily made at home in bulk, saving money over commercially bought and packaged trail mix. Be sure to add plenty of nuts, raisins and even some fatty items like chocolate chips and M&Ms to add additional calories.

Most dietitians agree that breakfast and lunch are the two most important meals of the day with breakfast being the most important. Even though this is true, it is hard for many people to get motivated to eat in the morning and the idea of setting up a stove to cook a large meal can be tough. For this reason, pack along some good quality dry cereal to eat without milk, a selection of dried fruit and even some packs of instant flavored oatmeal for a quick hot meal by just adding boiled water. By starting off your day right you will have much more energy to climb and stalk game.

For staying hydrated, most backcountry hunter's stick to good old water, but if you like a change or the water has a slight "taste" to it, pack along some individual flavor packs. I like those that use artificial sweetener as it takes very little of this lightweight sweetener compared to sugar, keeping weight and bulk to a minimum. Items like Tang have a lot of sugar already in them making them heavy as well as not the best energy fuel. However individual packets of Propel for example, weigh next to nothing, taste great and are packed with vitamins.

As a final note it is also a good idea for backcountry hunters to pack some small containers of garlic salt and pepper along with a few wraps of aluminum foil and even a collapsible metal forked stick (the modern day answer to the wire coat hanger). If game is taken – there is nothing more satisfying than enjoying a tenderloin steak broiled over an open fire. Use the metal forked stick and the spices to grill it to perfection.

To remain comfortable in all types of weather, hunters must layer to stay warm. Here the author is with a late season upper Midwest whitetail. The weather didn't rise above the teens all week, but even sitting on a treestand from morning to dark the author stayed warm.

CHAPTER 6

Dressed for Success

When it comes to serious big game hunting, dressed for success is more than a catch phrase. It is a way of life that needs to be taken seriously. It is the difference between staying warm, comfortable and dry or being soaking wet, cold and miserable. It often is the deciding factor between staying in the field until last light, or packing up early and heading back to camp. It can mean the difference between spending the entire trip hunting hard or lounging around camp by the fire. And in some extreme cases it can mean the difference between life and death. Dressing for success on a big game hunt is surely more than a fashion statement it is a serious part of the overall experience and can make or break a hunt.

PLANNING FOR YOUR HUNT

Since every big game hunt differs dramatically in its requirements, physical hardship, luggage and/or weight limitations, temperature range and physical exertion it is nearly impossible to define one set of apparel that is right for every situation. Throw in the anomaly that some guys are comfortable wearing a light fleece jacket when the temperature drops below freezing while others bundle up at the first hint of frost like they are going along with Shackleton to the South Pole and you can forget about me recommending one set of clothing that is ideal for all situations, simply put it doesn't exist.

Start by knowing your own tolerance for cold and heat, think about how much physical activity the hunt will entail and how you personally handle it and then move on to thinking about the physical conditions of the hunt.

As stated above, hunts vary widely. A hunter planning on spending all day perched in a tree on a cold November day in Canada for whitetails is going to require far different apparel than one spotting and stalking antelope on the plains in early October. But these are the extremes and consequently are easy to plan for. It is a pretty safe bet that you won't get too much cold weather on the early season antelope hunt or any warm weather on the November deer hunt. This makes planning accordingly a straight forward task.

Clothing planning gets more problematic during the middle season hunts, especially in mountainous country. One day it can be 70 degrees and sunny and the next morning you can wake up to snow and freezing temperatures. I have hunted all over, and I don't think I can name one place that experiences such wild temperature and weather swings as high mountain country in the fall. All this makes packing the right clothing all the more critical.

The only way I have found to stay comfortable in widely swinging conditions is to dress in layers. Layering does several things, it allows you to custom tailor the outfit for the temperature, it allows you to shed excess layers if the temperature or activity level increases and if done correctly with the right material it serves as a moisture management system, wicking moisture away from the body, where it would normally evaporate and cool the body, to the outer layers of the clothing keeping the wearer warmer and drier.

When designing a layering system start with the items closest to the skin. I personally always wear a base layer made from a high tech wicking material – both top and bottom. This base layer is generally thin, tight fitting and while does not provide a lot of direct warmth or insulation, reduces moisture next to the skin. It is the fundamental building block for staying warm. Polypropylene, a synthetic material, has been my choice of base layer for a long time, but other natural materials such as merino wool, and silk also work well.

After the base layer I put on an insulation layer – generally a thick long underwear type of garment. Long underwear varies in thicknesses from thin silk to heavy fleece "expedition" weight to quilted down. Select the one that best meets your hunt's requirements. If it is a normal fall hunt I will wear just a mid-weight set of long underwear tops and bottoms over my lightweight base layer and am fine, but if the weather threatens to be cold, I select the heavier fleece models or even thin quilted down if I plan to be very sedentary.

The middle clothing (often called "layering clothes") comes next. The purpose of this layer is to create an airspace, which retains warm air near the body. I like windproof fleece, wool, or down in a jacket or a vest. My choice between these three materials really depends upon how cold it is, and if I am trying to keep weight and size to a minimum (down is the lightest and most packable of all the insulating materials, but does have some drawbacks).

After the layering clothes it is time to choose an outer shell. If I know the hunt is going to be extremely cold and my activities relatively sedentary I will pick a waterproof, windproof, insulated parka and bibs. I feel an extra long parka combined with bibs is the best combination as the extra length creates an overlapping insulated area around your mid section and kidneys. This is extremely important for retaining core body heat, which in turn keeps fingers and toes warm.

If I don't anticipate the weather being extremely cold, I wear a noninsulated, but windproof and waterproof parka and bib or jacket and pant combo most of the time. I have hunted in this combination with temperatures well down into the single digits and as high as the low 70's by shedding inner layers. The nicest thing about this system is the flexibility. If the weather is warm and raining, you can store the inner insulating layer and even the long underwear inside your pack and just wear the wicking base layer and waterproof outer layer to stay dry and comfortable. When the weather turns cold or when you

By wearing several layers comprised of a wicking layer, an insulation layer and an outer water and windproof layer hunters can be ready for all weather situations.

stop hiking you can put all the insulating layers back on and remain comfortable for several hours of inactivity.

HEADWEAR

Insulated headwear is probably one of the best ways to regulate overall body core temperature. It is said that as much as 30% of the body's heat escapes through the head, so managing this area with the right clothing is imperative. For general hunting in warm conditions I don't give it much thought, generally wearing a baseball style cap to keep sun out of my eyes, but as soon as the temperature becomes even slightly chilly I prefer a waterproof insulated head covering. This may be in the form of a baseball style Gore-Tex/Thinsulate hat or more traditionally it is a wool stocking cap. Whatever I choose it must have good insulating properties and be cut in a fashion that covers the back of my neck and ears.

If it is raining, a hat with a wide brim all the way around like a cowboy hat or a waxed cotton packer-style hat works well for keeping rain from your face and running down your neck where it chills your whole body.

FEET AND HANDS

For keeping the feet and hands warm I first consider my core body temperature. One of the body's built-in survival traits is to shut down blood to extremities when cold to maintain the core body temperature for the vital organs. If I have a problem keeping my hands and feet warm I put on more layers around the midsection and wear a warmer hat. Then I concentrate on covering my hands and feet. For my feet I generally wear two pairs of socks, a lightweight liner sock made of silk and a heavy merino wool over sock. After hiking into an area where I plan to stay for a while many times I take my boots off, and change both these pairs of socks with fresh dry ones from my pack. This eliminates a lot of the cold causing moisture before your body has a chance to cool down. For gloves I like glomitts (glove mitten combos), the fingers stay warmer than with gloves and by pulling back the top mitten portion you have the manual dexterity of exposed fingers making it ideal for shooting a rifle or bow. If I am spending a lot of time in a stationary position like a deer stand I will often not wear gloves, but use an insulated muff around my waist. With a couple of Heat Factory chemical heat packs inside the muff my bare hands will stay very warm and ready for action when the moment of truth arrives.

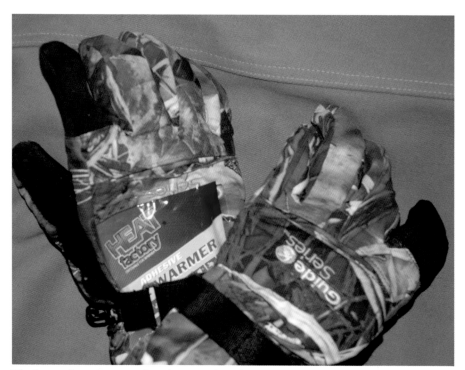

The key to keeping your hands warm is to keep your core temperature warm, but heat packs inside quality gloves also help keep your fingers flexible.

MATERIALS

Like many other items in the hunting industry the materials we use for outdoor clothing has made revolutionary strides since World War II. Pre WWII hunters didn't have many synthetics and their choices were pretty much limited to wool, down, leather, cotton and silk. Today hunters have hundreds of material choices with more coming out of labs every day. In many cases these materials are excellent for a select purpose and can replace materials of yesteryear, but a lot of hunters know, natures own "home grown" items are still in use and excelling even in today's world of synthetic textiles. Below is a run down of the pros and cons of most of the more common materials available to outdoors enthusiasts.

Wool

Nothing is more classic than an old picture of turn of the century deer hunters clad in red and black-checkered wool mackinaws. Those old time hunters knew wool kept out the cold, wet or dry, and it still does today. Wool is an excellent choice for keeping hunters warm afield and it has many advantages and only a few drawbacks. First

Wool is one of the oldest and most proven hunting garments. It blocks the wind, retains heat when wet and serves as an excellent insulator. Newer wool garments have successfully laminated with a waterproof membrane making possibly the perfect clothing.

off, wool is an excellent insulator, and it is one of the best materials at retaining heat when wet. It does a fair job of blocking wind, especially in the heavier weights, but still breathes extremely well wicking moisture away and out of the garment. But wool can be heavy both on the scale and on the wallet. Premium wool manufacturers get top dollar for their garments so it may not fit the budget. In addition wool is hard to make waterproof. However in very recent years it has been laminated with other materials, coated and treated to be water resistant and in some cases waterproof.

Down

Natural down, plucked from prime northern geese, is hard to beat when it comes to weight versus warmth insulation. It has one of the highest lofts of all insulation. It insulates extremely well when properly used in a garment and weighs very little. If it weren't for its high cost and nearly complete loss of insulating properties when wet it may be the ultimate insulator. Even so, when I am looking to go light on a trip or have limited packing space one of my most often used garments is a premium northern goose down vest. It packs up inside its own pocket stuff sack, takes up about as much space as a rolled up pair of heavy wool socks and as long as it is worn under a waterproof outer layer has always kept me very warm.

Cotton/Canvas

Every year in some camp I see a hunter heading afield with a cotton undershirt, cotton long underwear as a base layer or denim jeans and to be honest I just shake my head and wonder why. Cotton for most hunting purposes is a really bad idea. It has nearly no insulating properties by itself, is not waterproof or even resistant in its natural state. When wet it loses any insulating properties it may have had and wicks moisture about on par with a stone. With the very limited exception of some of the waxed cottons used as an outer shell, such as the Filson products, or for very early season warm, day hunts (early season archery deer and antelope hunts come to mind) avoid cotton when it comes to most serious back country adventures.

Silk

Silk is a natural fiber derived from the silk worm and has a long history in garment making. It is not used as much anymore due to high manufacturing costs and cheaper synthetics that essentially provide the same benefits. Silk is still a viable option for sock liners and base layer type clothing because it is comfortable to wear and wicks moisture well.

Gore-Tex

At one time Gore-Tex had the patent and subsequently the market on waterproof-breathable membrane material. In recent years as the patent has expired several other companies have introduced their own waterproof breathable membranes that work as well at a lower cost. This section covers all waterproof-breathable membrane materials. The theory behind all of these products is that a synthetic "rubbery" membrane is laminated or "hung" inside a garment, which has billions of small holes in it. The holes are large enough to let out water vapor generated from your body, while small enough to keep out water droplets from the outside. In theory this works well and has literally changed the way we look at waterproof garments. This material can be used in conjunction with a wide array of other materials creating a soft, quiet, flexible garment that is waterproof. As far as the breathability is concerned, this is the only flaw. The only serious downside is, that while technically breathable, none of the membranes are highly breathable and moisture may and often does collect inside the garment. Better than rubber or PVC products, breathable membranes are still not perfect, but they are the best available to date. As a side note, many of the manufacturers today recognize this problem and create garments with wicking liners to get the moisture away from the skin as well as incorporate ventilation zippers to allow excess moisture to escape.

Rubber

Rubber has been around for a long time, but with the addition of other waterproof options has fallen out of favor. It still has its place in the hunting fields. For really wet weather nothing works quite as well as a heavy-duty outer layer of commercial grade rubber bibs and parka. Rubber doesn't absorb any moisture, which weighs other garments down, and dries completely and quickly when hung in any tent with modest heat. This is something that cannot be said for more modern laminated waterproof membrane garments as they are generally bonded to a fleece nap material that absorbs water. I found this out the hard way on an Alaska spring bear hunt. My waterproof breathable membrane garments did keep me dry, but were still wet on the outside, cold, clammy and heavy the next day (the little stove in the wall tent didn't circulate enough heat to even come close to drying them out). The guide's all rubber suits were completely dry. For quartering or packing game and capes, rubber bibs don't absorb blood or grime and can quickly be washed off with a few handfuls of stream water.

The downside to rubber is that it rots, it is heavy, it is not very flexible, and it will feel cold and clammy to the touch.

When you're spending the day afield hunting that dream trophy animal, today's fabrics can keep you comfortable and warm, making the experience that much more enjoyable.

SCENT CONTROL

The topic of scent control clothing has long been examined among trophy whitetail hunters, but it is not often discussed when it comes to western hunting. I think there are several reasons for this. To begin with, when hunting whitetails a hunter is generally sneaking into a deer's core living area where scent contamination is readily detected. Further, whitetail hunters will stay in that core area for a long time allowing scent to permeate. Finally, controlling scent is much easier in the whitetail woods than on a western mountain. Most whitetail hunters are doing day hunts where they can return home or to a hotel at night, rewash their clothing, repack it in scent proof bags and shower themselves. This is not the case with most western hunts. Most western hunters don't have the luxury or recharging scent containing clothing, or showering and combined with the sheer physical nature of the hunt, perspiration is a major problem. However, under the right circumstances, western hunters could take some notes from their eastern hunting brethren and practice better scent elimination. For pure spot and stalk hunting with a rifle it is probably not necessary, but for early season archery rut hunting for elk, bow hunting for mule deer or ambushing tactics for either, good scent control will go along way towards getting the perfect shot. Since showering up with scent eliminating soap may not be feasible on a western hunt, hunters should look at utilizing some of the newer varieties of antimicrobial base layer clothing that essentially neutralizes bacteria before it can start to smell. Keeping a scent blocking outer layer packed in a scent proof bag to be put on just before a final stalk may mean the difference between securing a trophy, or going home empty handed. Don't forget scent-eliminating sprays which used on footwear and outer garments throughout a hunt can help cut down on ambient smell. I prefer Scent Blocker White Lighting as it comes in a convenient 16-ounce spray bottle and works extremely well at eliminating scent.

Scent control is a multi-pronged approach. Start by washing all clothes as well as showering with scent eliminating soap and shampoo. Use scent free deodorant then wear a Scent Blocker activated carbon suit.

CHAPTER 7

Care of Game from Field to Home

I speak with countless hunters each year who want to hunt big game in the western wilderness without a guide either as a challenge or from financial limitations. In itself there is nothing wrong with this and for a sense of self-satisfaction everything right with it. However, in order to do it yourself successfully, you need to have the basic skills at your disposable. One of the most necessary skills, and surprising one of the most lacking is field care of game. I

When hunting deep in the backcountry everything must be packed in and out on your back. This means hunters must know how to fully process game in the field to reduce it to manageable sections.

may be wrong, but I don't believe this was true a generation or two ago. With increased urbanization of hunters, as well as a shrinking degree of true wilderness, many hunters have never learned the vital skill of caring for their own game. Many of today's hunters simply load a deer into the back of a truck and take it to the butcher. While many hunters know how to gut a big game animal, it is surprising to see how many do not. Very few know how to properly cape, quarter and debone an animal. These skills are not necessary for those who have a vehicle at their disposal; they are vital for the backcountry hunter who only has his two legs to get game out of the field. Even if the area is road accessible, knowing how to quarter game and cape a hide is very important in the transportation process.

BASIC FIELD CARE OF MEAT

Gutting

The very first and most basic step to taking care of game meat is removing the entrails and vital organs, generally known as "gutting". This is a simple process and shouldn't take more than 15 minutes, even on a large animal such as an elk. Lay the animal on its back, it helps to have a partner to hold its legs, but if you are by yourself, lengths of cord tied from each leg to trees will help immensely. Make

Knowing how to gut an animal is vital for all hunters regardless of location or species. Here the author's girlfriend gets her first lesson.

an incision from the anal region to the sternum (if you don't intend to mount the head, cutting through the sternum makes the job a bit easier). Cut around the diaphragm (the muscle membrane that separates the vital organs from the entrails). Reach up into the chest cavity as far as possible and sever the windpipe. Go back down to the pelvis region and separate the pelvic bone with either a stout knife or a small saw (some companies make small pelvic saws that work ideal). And finally sever the hide around the anus. At this point all of the vitals and entrails can be stripped from the body. Separate the heart and liver from the other organs and reserve for use. Prop the chest cavity open with a couple of branches and roll a couple of logs under the body to allow air to circulate and for the time being you are done.

Skinning

I prefer to hang and skin the animal very shortly after gutting if the weather is warm. If the animal can be brought to camp whole it is best to leave the hide on until then to keep dirt and debris out of the meat. If the animal must be packed out in pieces skip the skinning and gutting and go right to quartering. However if you are doing a traditional skinning job, hang the animal by its rear legs by making an incision at the hock joint between the Achilles tendon and the leg bone. Spreading the legs eases the job, but not an absolute necessity. Traditionally a device called a gambrel is used. A length of wood will serve, or use two separate ropes. Hoist the animal to about head high – you may need to adjust up or down depending upon where you are working. If you plan on keeping the cape and mounting the animal cut the hide well behind the shoulder about level with the middle of the sternum. Cut all the way around the animal. Next make a cut up the center of the back right along the spine from the mid point to the base of the skull. Now the cape portion of the skin can be peeled off the back, down the forelegs and the neck. Separate the skull from the spine by cutting through the tissue between the base of the skull and the last vertebrae. Leave the final facial caping of the skull for later, but don't wait too long as in warm weather the hair will slip from around the eyes, nose and ears.

Now that the front cape is off, the rear portion of the hide can be split down the inside of the rear legs and skinned in a normal fashion. After skinning I cover the carcass with either cheesecloth or canvas game bag. This last step is important for keeping flies off of the meat but still allowing air to circulate so a protective crust dries on the outside of the carcass.

After the skinned carcass has had sufficient time to cool down, generally overnight in average fall weather, you may want to quarter your game. If you can take the animal to the butcher by vehicle, you will not have to quarter. If you flew to an area or plan to ship the meat home, it will have to be reduced to quarters or even deboned to save weight. Quartering is a simple process and shouldn't take more than a half an hour.

I prefer to have the carcass hanging just as it was for skinning. Start with the front legs. Cut them off at the knee with a saw or by using a knife in between the bones at the joint. Insert the knife into the "armpit" region of the front quarter and slice the muscle between the leg and the rib cage. While pulling the leg away from the body and continuing to cut up towards the back, you can easily separate the front leg from the body. Repeat with the second front leg.

At this point you are at a natural transition to slice straight down along the spine from the front shoulders to the start of the rear legs. Do this on both sides of the spine and remove the backstraps from the animal. Much like filleting a fish these excellent chunks of meat will roll away from the backbone/rib cage with very little pressure. On the opposite side of the spine (inside the body cavity) two smaller backstraps called tenderloins will be found, remove them the same way as the main backstraps.

Fleshing and salting the hide from your trophy is important in maintaining quality, but it sure is a lot of work.

Before removing the rear quarters take the time to fillet the neck, rib and brisket meat from the bone as it is easy to get at this meat while the animal is still hanging. The final step is to remove the two hind quarters. Start by cutting through the meat where the rear quarter meets to the spine. Cut back along the pelvis until the ball joint is reached. By over extending the joint the ball will pop free of the socket. Cut through any tendons or left over muscle and the rear quarter will come free. Cut the lower leg from the quarter below the hock joint with a saw. Repeat with the final rear quarter and the job will be complete.

QUARTERING IN THE FIELD

If you are deep in the backcountry and on foot you may choose to skip the traditional method of skinning and gutting and go right to quartering. Since you will have limited equipment this is almost always done on the ground. I like to carry a small square of plastic in my pack to lay all the meat on to keep it clean. Laying the animal on its back, much like you would start the gutting job. However instead of gutting, carefully cut through the skin from the rear knee (hock joint) to the crotch of the animal. Cut completely around the joint and pull the skin down towards the body completely exposing the quarter. Remove this quarter as described in the quartering section.

If you want a full shoulder mount, be sure to leave plenty of hide for the taxidermist to work with. When caping, a full incision should be made around the animal then split up the back to the base of the skull.

If you're hunting terrain like this, you'll want to quarter your animal out before attempting to drag it. Too many hunters are injured, or worse, when they attempt to drag their animal over too far of a distance, or in terrain they can't handle.

Repeat this procedure with the other quarter. If you do not want to save the cape, skin up the front legs to the armpit and remove the front quarters as previously described.

To save the cape, make the incision around the body and one incision from the tailbone straight up the spine to the base of the neck. Peel the rear section (often referred to as the backskin) back off the rear far enough to access the backstraps and the front cape skinned down around the neck. At this point the back straps and front legs can be removed. Finish up by removing the neck, rib and brisket meat and you are almost done. The only trick to this method of field dressing is retrieving the tenderloins. The easiest method is to reach inside the body cavity through the top where the back straps used to reside (behind the last rib). The tenderloins can then be removed, leaving the guts and main carcass intact and left at the site.

Roll the cape onto itself and pack it out with the rack. The rest of the meat can be packaged into individual game bags for transport or placed into an internal frame pack.

Another step some hunters take (where allowed by law) is to de-bone all of the quarters to reduce weight. This is relatively simple to do and if you have a long way to travel can significantly reduce your overall load.

This is not a high fence hunt, just a very lucky situation. This is the easiest elk pack job the author has ever experienced. Luckily, the bull died in an area of a ranch where a truck could drive. The author has packed out his fair share of elk quarters over miles of rough terrain and was not going to look a gift horse or elk in the mouth.

Taking Photographs of the kill scene

If you butcher an animal in a remote location and pack out the quarters or de-boned meat it is not a bad idea to take a series of photos of the process, the kill site and the carcass left behind. In certain states where this type of field processing is a common practice, laws are very strict on wanton waste of game meat (as they should be) and have stringent guidelines on how much meat should be brought out. These laws are designed to stop unethical hunters from doing a sloppy job of field butchering or claiming parts were blood shot, etc. so they won't have to carry them out. I am all for enforcing these laws. My only concern is when the bad guys tarnish the good guys and we are looked upon in a poor light. If a game warden desires he can make you hike back into the kill site and show him the carcass if he believes wanton waste may be an issue. For this reason, taking multiple photos of every step of the process including the bones of the carcass is a good idea and may help prove you took all edible meat out with you. Even if you are never questioned, it may save you miles of walking.

Getting it all Back Home

Hunters spend a lot of time planning a dream hunting trip far from home for a long desired big game species. No amount of time is too great in doing the preliminary research, apply for coveted tags, scouting, talking to locals and landowners and laying the groundwork for success. The anticipation is a very pleasurable part of the overall experience. In fact, many spend so much time planning that they forget to figure out what must happen after they are successful. While easily avoidable, you wouldn't be the first hunter trying to jam quarters of an elk into the impossibly small, carpeted hatchback of a rented mini-SUV and scratching your head trying to figure out how to get it all home. While there really is no one single blueprint for taking care of your trophy and meat after the shot on a remote hunt, here are some pointers and suggestions for getting it all back home.

As most hunters know the meat from a big game animal is as much of a trophy as the hide or horns. It is the symbolic lifeblood of why we hunt. It is nutritious, satisfying and often just plain delicious. It serves as a tangible reminder of the hunt and of past good times. However sometimes when far from home getting meat back to where one can enjoy it requires a lot of planning and a very significant cost.

The difficulty involved with getting meat back home depends upon the size of the species, mode of travel, time of year and the amount of meat and trophies you need to bring home.

The first major factor to consider is how you got to the hunting area. If you drove, getting all the meat back is a pretty simple affair. If you flew it becomes more difficult and a lot more expensive.

Mobile hunters with their own vehicle have an easy go of getting it all back home as long as they made the right preparations before they left. For the smaller species such as antelope, mountain goat, sheep, deer, etc. the needed equipment is pretty straightforward. The bigger the species, such as moose, elk and caribou, the more planning is required. For smaller game all you will need is one to two large coolers. You can either bring one from home or you can buy one at the destination after you get your animal. All you will need then is a good sharp knife, a field gambrel, some plastic bags and dry or wet ice. Every area has different regulations as to when and where you can process meat, and since these regulations change with some regularity it is impossible to cover this indetail here. The best bet is to contact the local regulatory agency well before the hunt for a detailed description of how and when you can cut up meat. Some of this information will also be covered in the hunting regulations. In some cases the animal can be field butchered i.e. skinned, quartered and deboned. In other cases the animal can only be quartered. In some cases proof of sex must remain attached to a major body part. If a particular area requires that the animal must remain intact and identifiable, get the skin off as quickly as possible and get a breathable cloth bag over the meat. This will go a long way towards avoiding deterioration of the meat.

Keeping meat cool really depends upon the time of the year and weather conditions. I personally would think nothing of transporting a whole elk (skin removed of course) several days in the back of a pickup truck if the temperature was around freezing at night and no higher than mid 40's in the day. Most experts agree several days to a week of aging under these conditions are ideal for proper flavor and tenderness in game. The key is to make sure the entire animal gets cooled down in the beginning by removing the hide then making sure there are no "hot spots" where the animal is laying on its back for an extended time or between the rear hams. The easiest way to avoid this is to allow air to circulate. Separate the legs with a forked branch and place a couple of 2x4s cross ways under the carcass to keep air flowing underneath.

However if an animal is taken in the early season when daytime temperatures soar into the 70's and often above, leaving the animal whole is not an option – it will spoil in short order. In this situation depending upon local laws once again, I prefer to quarter the animal and get the meat cooled down on ice if possible. While some hunters don't like to get game meat wet (and therefore use dry ice) I have never found that wet meat has affected the taste or texture of game. If you plan to process the game meat yourself back home, quartering the animal, and putting it on ice will work fine for several days as long as you refill the ice and drain the water periodically. If you plan to have the animal butchered by others it is often better to take it to a local butcher in the hunting area. Often you can pay a little extra and they will butcher an animal in a day or so – this is especially true in the earlier season before the big rush of game animals has them back logged (busy to get to your animal in a couple of days). If you have a local butcher process your game it will be frozen solid when you pick it up. Packed tightly in a quality cooler with dry ice it will stay frozen until you arrive home.

All the above scenarios best apply to hunters with their own vehicle. For hunters traveling on commercial airlines, the issue of meat transportation is a bit more difficult. There are three basic options for airborne hunters. Take the meat on the plane as checked luggage, take the meat to a local butcher and have it shipped home when it is completed or donate it to a local food shelter or one of the various "Hunters Feeding the Hungry" programs.

If you choose to bring it with you on the airline there will generally be an up charge per extra bag. A cooler or waxed, liquid-proof meat packing box will count as one bag. If you choose to use a cooler all ice must be removed (some airlines allow a limited amount of dry ice to stay in the cooler, but check on the airline web site beforehand) so the meat needs to be properly cooled down before shipping. If meat is cold I have never experienced a problem with spoilage, as flights almost anywhere in the continental United States are less than four hours. However if you get delayed or have an extremely long layover, spoilage may become a problem. All packages should be labeled as perishable and the airline made aware of its contents.

By far the easiest way to transport meat home is to take it to a local butcher, have them package and freeze it and have it next day airmailed to your residence. This is the easiest, but also the most costly. Depending upon the size of the animal and the distance shipped, figure on two to several hundred dollars in shipping charges.

The final method of dealing with game meat on an out of state hunt is to donate all or part of it to a food bank or charity. Depending upon the state this process may differ. In some locales hunters need to pay the processing charge and fill out a form, in others there is little or no fee. Check into these programs ahead of time and keep all the contact info handy in the event you get an animal. While most hunters like to enjoy the meat, part of the hunt has always been sharing with those less fortunate than you and donating meat is still a great way to do that.

PREPARING TROPHIES FOR TRAVEL

Preparing the trophy for transport back home, also, depends not only upon the time of year and method of transportation, but the size of the trophy and type of mount desired also plays a roll.

If the temperatures are cold and you have the space in a vehicle, skin the animal from behind the shoulder to the base of the skull straight up the back of the neck. Remove the head from the body at the juncture of the last vertebrae. If the temperature is hot you may want to cape the hide completely off the skull and flesh it accordingly (see side bar for more information). Once the cape is removed it can either be heavily salted, it can be frozen or it can be kept in a cooler with dry ice. Depending upon how you want to mount the animal you can either separate the rack from the skull and dispose of the skull or you can leave the rack attached to the skull in the case of a European style mount. If you are not doing a European mount and have cut the antlers from the skull think about splitting the skull plate. If the antlers are large like a caribou or elk, it makes transport much easier and affordable. However keep in mind that by doing so it disqualifies the animal for any record book entry. If this is important to you, do not ever split the antlers apart from each other. If you don't care about record books, split them immediately, wrap each antler in bubble wrap and then nestle and tape together.

The biggest factor to dealing with a trophy mount is just planning ahead. If you plan to use a taxidermist in your home area, visit that taxidermist ahead of time. They will tell you exactly how they like to receive trophies, will give you their shipping information and possibly show you their preferred way to cape an animal for the best possible mount. Once you have this information it is easy to box up the cape and rack from nearly anywhere you are hunting and overnight it to the taxidermist. If you don't have a local taxidermist another great option is to find a taxidermist in the region you will

Moose are big animals and packing one out is the hard part. Luckily we had ARGO all-terrain vehicle to help us get this big boy out and into a cooler. ATVs are a great tool for packing out meat. Just be sure to check local regulations on the use.

be hunting. Check their references, prices, availability, etc. and make contact with them ahead of time. If you get an animal, it is as easy as dropping it off with them, letting them do the cape work, mount the animal and ship it home after it is done. While it will cost a bit more to ship the finished mount back to your home state the headache factor is reduced considerably. Like dealing with meat, check all laws in the area you are hunting to make sure you do not end up in unknowing violation. Some states and regions have varying laws on how and when you can sever the head from a game animal and in some areas that have serious diseases such as CWD animals must be tested before being cut up and taken out of state.

NEEDED SUPPLIES

After spending a long and trying evening in Anchorage, Alaska attempting to ship a rack from a recently shot caribou through the only 24 hour US Post Office I have ever visited and repeatedly needing various packing supplies I decided in the future to always bring along some trophy preparation material for shipping racks back home.

Regardless of the method of travel or what you plan on doing with the trophy or meat, a certain amount of supplies are necessary to have with you. I now bring the following with me on trips where I may have to ship racks.

- A sheet of clear plastic to wrap the skull for waterproofing
- Bubble wrap
- A couple of plastic garbage bags
- Shipping tape
- One-inch sections of common garden hose for the points on the rack to comply with shipping regulations.
- Zip Ties
- Pre Printed, plastic laminated cards with my address on it
- A few wet naps to wipe blood off the rack (even if dried, I have had racks rejected from an airlines/shipping company due to visible blood).
- Shrink wrap

Plan how you are going to ship antlers back home before you go on your trip. Airlines, private shipping companies and the US post office

Transporting meat across state and country borders

With the spread of CWD (Chronic Wasting Disease) and Mad Cow disease transporting game animals across state and county lines is not as simple as it used to be. The regulations vary widely from place to place and really change when an outbreak is suspected. Little can be written about the current state of transporting game other than to be aware this threat exists and local game department should be contacted for exact instructions before a hunt is undertaken. If your trip is outside of the US get the current information from your outfitter or through USFW before departing. See the back of this book for all state and federal wildlife organization contact info.

all have different shipping policies that may be subject to change. It is best to know the details before you go. In addition, in the cases of oversized racks (caribou and moose in particular) keep in mind you may need to split the rack for easier transport. However by doing so it eliminates them from being officially scored. If racks are to be shipped whole, put a support bar (forked branch, cut off broom handle, etc.) between the antlers to keep the skull from splitting. This is especially important on species like mule deer, caribou and elk.

Bringing your own freezer

Working as a booking agent I remember my easiest client to deal with. Upon our first booking I asked how he preferred to travel to the hunting destination and had he given any thought to meat transportation back home? He replied he planned on driving and towing a large enclosed trailer with all of his gear, including a large chest freezer and generator to power it! This gentleman had obviously been down this road before and knew how tough transporting game can be. If you have the ability and the time to drive to your hunting destination there is no easier way to bring home meat and trophies than in a freezer in a trailer. While not practical for everyone, given the opportunity I would personally choose this method every time!

A good pack frame is VITAL as is a good knife for taking care of game when you're deep in the field.

Full Caping

If you are on a remote hunt and have to pack game out or if the weather is hot and you are worried about losing the cape through hair slippage it is necessary to fully cape any animal you wish to mount. If you have never done it before, at first it seems like a daunting task, but once you have done it a few times you will find it is extremely easy to do and takes very little time. I have found the best way to cape an animal is to go down to your local taxidermists during regular deer season and ask if you can watch how they do it. Usually this is readily agreed to, especially if you inform them of your plans of going on a big game hunt yourself and will want them to do the taxidermy work. Watching the process done is always much easier than reading about it, but in lieu of that here are the basics of caping.

Assuming you have already cut the animal up the back to the base of the antlers, removed the head and major cape from the body, start by making a Y slit from the base of the skull to the base of each antler. Use a very sharp caping knife to separate the hide from the base of each antler/horn working all the way around the base until free. It is very important to leave no hide on the pedicles of the antler. From this point peel the hide off the skull down to the base of the ears. Cut through the cartilage of the ears where they meet the skull. Keep skinning until the eyes are reached. Before you get too close, put your non-knife hand in the eye to use as a gauge, very carefully cut up to your finger, leaving plenty of skin around the eye socket for the taxidermist to work with. From this point continue skinning towards the mouth and nose separating the skin from the skull as close to the skull as possible, this will ensure there is plenty of skin around the mouth for the taxidermist to use. Finally cut through the septum of the nose as close to the skull as possible. At this point the cape will be removed from the skull. The antlers can now be sawed off the skull and the skull discarded. The final steps in caping are to split the lips, eyelids and separate the ear from the cartilage membrane. For doing the ears I recommend bringing along a commercial ear separator, available from most taxidermy supply stores. It will make the job much easier. Be sure to do these last steps very carefully and do not cut through the outside of the skin or it will show on the final mount. Once this is all completed, rub the skin side of the entire cape down with liberal amounts of salt paying special attention to the ears, eyes and lips. Fold the skin onto itself and allow the salt to work into the skin and you have a cape that will last until you get it to the taxidermist.

CHAPTER 8

Backcountry Survival

I was following a herd of elk through Washington's Cascade Mountains, bow hunting in early September, I had been on them since lunch when they came storming right through our tent camp. I grabbed my bow and took off in pursuit, thinking they would slow down within a few hundred yards. Not thinking I would be following them so far and caught up in the excitement of the moment I left my day pack with all my survival tools, emergency clothes, fire starters, water and food sitting on my cot. That was nearly six hours before. Now the evening shadows were growing long and the air was taking on a decidedly non-summer feel. My sweat-soaked short-sleeved cotton shirt was not providing a lot of warmth.

While catching the elk had been my goal, my only thought now was to get out of the backcountry and back to camp or find an old logging road or some form of human contact before dark. I hustled up the ridgeback I was hiking to get to the top for a better view. The eastern slope of the Cascades are notoriously easy to get lost in as they are covered in semi-dwarfed ponderosa pines which make lateral visibility nearly impossible. Upon reaching the top I was granted an awesome 360 degree panoramic view of miles upon miles of country, and while gorgeous it was very intimidating as there was not one road, camp, house or town visible, which made this 22 year old hunter feel rather small.

Feeling panic set in I decided to sit right down on the nearest rock and assess the situation and take stock of my supplies, which was easy enough as I had next to nothing! I had on one cotton shirt and one cotton set of pants, one bow, four arrows with broadheads and a set of boots. No knife, no compass or GPS and no matches – all

Even if you don't plan on being away from camp very long, go prepared for any eventuality. Little things like a bull elk may lead you farther than you anticipated.

my supplies were in the daypack. However the good news was I couldn't be more than 10 miles from camp. On average over flat ground I walk about 3 miles per hour, although I had been walking for several hours, much of it had been slow going. I wasn't going to starve to death, there was plenty of water in several small streams that may or may not have diseases, something I would have to worry about later, and the weather, while chilly, was not expected to be life-threateningly cold.

I gathered some soft evergreen bows and piled them around the base of a large ponderosa and covered them with heaping armloads of dry pine needles. Once a soft, warm bed was fashioned I curled up for a long fitful sleep under the stars.

As soon as the sun went down and the darkness closed in I was able to make out the flickering lights of town 20 some miles off in the distance and from there could generally make out the direction of camp. At first light I ascertained which valley camp was in and with a growling stomach headed off. By midmorning I was back at camp. That was and still is my only getting lost story where I have had to spend an unplanned night lost in the outdoors. Sure I have been turned around a time or two since then, but due to proper planning and having a compass and GPS as well as maps I have always been able to find my way back to camp.

I have often thought about that night when planning future trips. While my ordeal was completely minor and luckily the weather was very cooperative, what if it hadn't been? What if I had sprained an ankle? Or had been hunting just a little bit later in the year when a nightly freeze or snowstorm was more common? The point is I got lucky and since I have never considered myself overly lucky, I have planned much better and have since taken more precautions when heading afield.

MAKE A PLAN AND LET OTHERS KNOW WHERE YOU ARE

When I arrived back in camp the following morning my hunting partners were a bit worked up. They had lost an entire morning of hunting while looking for me – expecting to find my body at the bottom of one of the ravines. While I was thankful someone was out looking for me, I was also ashamed that my lack of planning caused others some hardship. Since then we have made sure others in the camp knew what direction we were heading and when we planned to return. This is basic common sense that often gets overlooked. In addition to this we now have a rule to not go looking for anyone until 24 hours after last seeing him or her. At first this seems rather callous, but often when guys are hunting far ranging elk and they get a shot at dark, they may choose to stay right there living out of their pack waiting for first light to blood trail or in the event that they downed the animal wish to stay close by to protect the carcass from predators. By establishing this rule, there is never self induced pressure to hike out in the dark, possibly getting lost, spraining an ankle or hurting yourself just so hunting buddies don't worry. Every hunter knows he has 24 hours since last check in to make it back to camp before anyone will start to worry.

Go Prepared

As I described in the opening of this chapter, I was self admittedly ill prepared to be in the woods. Even though I left my pack in camp, I should have at least had a knife, a lighter and a candy bar in my hunting pockets. But an easier method is to always carry a well-stocked daypack or fanny pack. The first item that should be in every hunters pack is a GPS. If you don't already use one, get one and start, if you are like the millions of other hunters who regularly use them, you know what I am talking about. GPS technology has come a long way in the last 10 years. They are very easy to use, very durable and can cost as little as a few boxes of rifle cartridges. They can be as simple or as sophisticated as one wants, store thousands of waypoints, have color topo maps installed and in some instances can even be used as two way radios that allow you to communicate, and mark your position for a partner to find you.

As much as I use, trust and appreciate GPS units, there is still one percent of me that worries about batteries or electronic malfunctions and just plain likes to double check everything. For this reason I still bring a small compass in my pack along with several waterproof topo maps of the region "just in case" I need to double check my GPS. I haven't needed them so far, but the knowledge that they are there is always comforting.

If you are planning on staying out in the wilderness the amount of gear needed can be substantial and hard to carry, but if you bring just a few simple items in a small day pack or a fanny pack an unexpected stay can become a lot more comfortable as well as safe. In my pack I like to carry a couple of extra high-energy nutritional bars – they are not packed as "lunch," but always reside there in case of an emergency. They never go bad and only get used in a true emergency. I pack a lunch daily in addition to these bars to ensure they don't get consumed. While it takes days if not weeks to starve and the odds of ever getting lost for that long in the lower 48 are slim to none, it is much easier to concentrate, hike and even fall asleep with some food in your stomach. I also keep extra water purification tablets, a small first aid kit, an extra knife, whistle, signal mirror, several varieties of fire starters, waterproof matches/lighter/magnesium bar and an emergency space blanket. In addition to these necessities I like to bring a very small roll of 5mil clear plastic and some parachute cord. These items take up little space, weigh next to nothing and can be used for many tasks including building a waterproof shelter for the night.

A completely equipped day pack doesn't weigh that much and it can be a literal life saver should things go awry.

What's in your pockets?

While carrying a small pack with survival items is mandatory, I now carry a few items in my pockets as backup should I ever get separated from my pack. A floatplane pilot of mine lives by this rule. He has a complete waterproof floating survival kit in his plane, but you will never catch him flying anywhere without some basics in his pocket. This includes a sharp penknife, a lighter and possibly a round ball style compass safety pinned to his jacket. Hunters should do likewise. A small compass, knife, waterproof matches or lighter and a small whistle should always be at hand wherever you go.

While you should always carry a pack, as a back up plan it is always a good idea to have a small supply of gear stowed away in your pockets. Something as simple as a lighter and a ball type compass could save the day.

IF YOU GET LOST, PRIORITIZE

Too many lost people, when they eventually admit they are lost, start thinking about starving to death when they should be thinking about staying warm and dry. On average a human can live for about 30 days without food, 6 days without water and only a few hours without shelter/heat. This rule of thumb demonstrates how important shelter and fire are to a lost hunter. If you find yourself lost, forget about looking for water or food and concentrate on building a shelter and a fire. A shelter ideally will be located next to fuel for a fire and water to drink, but needs to always be located in a safe place, free from flash floods, avalanching snow or falling trees in high wind. After you have located a prospective site look for natural structures to help build a shelter; a cave, cliff face or a large down tree will all suffice. While structures vary by the material at hand, one of the most useful is a lean-to design utilizing the cliff face or downed tree as the main support. Use branches to establish a roof line and then cover with more tree limbs, bark, leaves or if you have it plastic sheeting. Once a shelter has been established, it is time to get a fire going. Place the fire at a safe distance in front of the shelter with a reflector shield behind it made from logs or rocks to bounce heat back into the shelter. Stack up plenty of dead and dry firewood and keep the fire going all night. After all of this has been done you can start looking for water and food.

FOOD AND WATER

Since most "lost" ordeals are over within 24 hours and even in the most remote country being stranded for more than two weeks would be very rare, I am not going to go into great length on procuring food. The odds of starving to death are very slim, however water can be a different issue. The human body needs 2-3 quarts of water a day to properly function and if not properly hydrated neither the body nor the mind work very well. Depending upon where you are hunting, water is often plentiful in the form of rain, falling snow, snow banks, ponds, lakes and streams. Rain and snow can be consumed right as it is, but lakes and rivers no matter how remote should be purified (with some limited exceptions such as springs at the source and high arctic country in the north and that is not 100% safe). Purification however is very simple, use commercial purification pills or boil for at least 5 minutes. If you do find yourself stranded in an arid region with no surface moisture, don't despair; water can be obtained by making a solar still. These stills will produce several pints of pure water a day and can literally be a life saver in an arid region. Start by digging a hole in the ground 3 feet deep and 4 feet in diameter. Put a water container in the center (jar, water bottle, cup, etc) cut fresh green foliage (even sage brush will work) and put it in the hole. Insert a length of rubber surgical tubing from your first aid kit into the jar and run it out of the hole. Cover the hole with plastic sheeting and seal with dirt and rocks around the outside. Place a single rock in the center of the sheeting to dimple it down towards the cup below. The heat of the day will cause the moisture inside the plants to evaporate; it will condense on the underside of the plastic and run "downhill" until it drips off the bottom into the cup. You can keep the still working by not breaking the seal and simply drinking the contents out of the cup through the surgical tubing straw.

FIRST AID KIT

I always have a small emergency first aid kit in my pack. Although rarely needed, it can be a life saver if you or someone in your party is injured. While necessary for emergencies, mine is also stocked with many items that make minor discomforts much more bearable and can often mean the difference between remaining comfortable enough to continue hunting or heading back to the doctor's office. Start with a basic commercial first aid kit. The small pouch comes in handy and most have clear plastic panels that allow for good organization of various items. Most will come stocked with a few Band-Aids, some gauze, a packet of aspirin, some medical tape, etc. I generally add to this assortment: some large gauze pads for larger wounds, an unbreakable bottle of iodine, a miniature soap for washing wounds, some alcohol based hand sanitizer, a small, one ounce plastic bottle of hydrogen peroxide, a hermetically sealed surgical stapler or suture kit (both these items need medical training to be used), a large bottle of 500 mg extra strength Tylenol or similar pain reliever. It is also a wise course of action to spend some time with your family doctor. Explain that you are putting together a medical kit for backcountry survival and see what medications he or she would recommend putting in the kit. Most will recommend and prescribe if necessary some form of anti-diarrhea medication, anti-infection and possibly sleep aids for travelers.

GETTING FOUND

Most experts agree that the best course of action for folks seriously lost is to stay put. If you have let others know approximately where you are going and when you are coming back sooner or later someone will find you. To help in their search, plan on using several items already brought along at your disposal to direct them to your spot. Basic methods include such items as a signal mirror used to shine people out of hearing range as well as in passing planes. Frequently blow a loud whistle, which will carry much farther than the human voice and is also much easier. Also starting a smoky fire and stomping patterns in the snow or sand will help searchers spot you. Anything you can do to draw attention to your position will help in a search effort. While these methods have been standbys for generations, some more modern items also can help get you found. Look at simple items such as a high intensity strobe light commonly used by downed airmen and sailors. They are small, lightweight and send out a very intense beam of light that can be seen for miles. Even a flashlight can be seen for miles at night. Three quick bursts periodically from your flashlight can help searchers locate your position. In addition to strobes and flashlights, modern electronics can also be a life saver. Obviously if your cell phone works, this is a great survival tool and is used many times each hunting

Personal Locator Beacons (PLBs) are becoming more and in small, lightweight and rugged enough to live in your pack virtually forever, they can beam a GPS signal to a satellite (much like a sat phone) which will alert emergency rescue services to your position.

Pocket Survival Book

Integrity House Publishing in Oregon makes a great pocket sized survival book that always resides in my pack. Measuring approximately 2.5 inches by 3 inches this 33 page book is one of the most complete survival/first aid books I have run across. Costing only a few dollars and printed on waterproof paper, this is a must have item for backcountry travelers. From topics and information for dealing with broken bones, heart attacks, bleeding, burns, CPR and hypothermia to building shelters, using a compass, to edible plants this book is like having a survival expert in your back pocket.

A pocket survival book is like having a survival expert with you at all times. It covers many topics from shelter building to gather edible food to dealing with a host of medical emergencies. Not to mention if you get bored at night while lost it makes good reading.

season by stranded, lost and injured hunters. But unfortunately in most cases in the back woods cell service is non-existent. For these areas it is not a bad idea to carry a satellite phone. Sat phones work nearly anywhere and are getting lighter and smaller all the time. They don't cost as much to purchase and use as many think, and can be rented for specific hunts. When I go to really remote areas and third world countries such as Africa I often bring a sat phone and have had great luck with their service.

When you have tried everything else – getting yourself out by GPS and compass, waiting for friends and family to find you, using smoke signals it may be time to pull the last resort – a PLB. Many hunters are not familiar with PLBs as they are relatively new to the consumer market, but pilots and seamen have been using them for years. PLB stands for Personal Locator Beacon and works by beaming a constant GPS distress signal to a satellite which sends it in turn to one of several emergency responders which can in turn pinpoint your location to several meters. These units are user friendly, affordable, easy and lightweight to pack and durable to all elements. Should everything else fail and you find your self in immanent danger of life or limb a PBL may be your best solution.

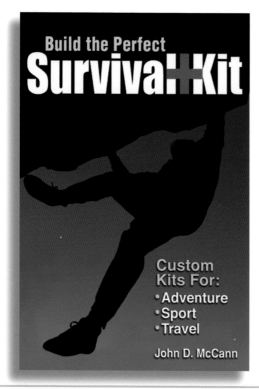

Also, Krause Publications that published the very book you have in your hands published a book by John McCann titled *Build the Perfect Survival* Kit. I consider this book essential reading for the backcountry hunter and is a good read for anyone going afield.

North America still offers many fine adventures for the traveling hunter. From trophy whitetails in your home state to bigger game out West, all it takes is a little planning to make it happen.

CHAPTER 9

Do It Yourself Big Game Species

This section is dedicated to the various North American big game species hunters can target without a guide. It is by design that there is little mention of the various Canadian big game species and only select species in Alaska as in both cases non-resident hunters are required to employee a guide. The whole point of this book is big game hunting on a budget. When mandatory guiding comes into play as it does in Canada and to a lesser degree Alaska, for most of us, the intended quarry moves out of the "budget" column and into the "unaffordable" column.

The species listed below are available for non-resident hunters and can be done cost effectively without a guide (with the limited Canadian exceptions). However, many of which are only available (as a budget species) with a highly-coveted drawn tag. Keep in mind every species has swings in population, trophy size and places are very likely to open or close down by the time the reader finds this. This is merely a guide to get you started down the right path.

WHITETAIL DEER

It is no secret that whitetail deer (Odocoileus Virginianus) are America's darling big game animal. More hunters currently pursue them than any other big game species in North America. There are countless reams of material and many books written covering virtually every aspect of whitetail deer hunting. I make no attempt to believe this short treatise on trophy whitetail deer is anywhere close to the material already in existence, but more of a current look at where trophy deer are coming from and how to access some of the best deer hunting in the country without breaking the budget.

Whitetails are America's darling hunting species and are the most commonly hunted big game animal from coast to coast. A few years and this guy will be a wall hanger.

While nearly every state in the lower 48 has a population of whitetail deer only a handful of states consistently put out trophy wild deer on a regular basis. Many states have high fence operations, but only fair chase hunts are covered in this book. Here is a look at some of the best places by region.

THE UPPER MIDWEST

The Upper Midwest may be the top trophy producing area for whitetails anywhere in the United States. The mixture of woods and edge cover combined with top food choices such as corn and soybeans have yielded massive bodies and even bigger racks. The insurgence of QDM (Quality Deer Management), on both public and private land, has created a situation where trophy-sized deer are becoming more and more common with records being broken every year. Setting records for whitetails is not a thing of the past, but a very real opportunity hunters have today and in the near future.

Whitetail just seem to get bigger and bigger. With QDM, good genetics and selective harvest this trend will continue. Look to the northern stretch of the Midwest for some of the best trophies, like this Wisconsin bruiser taken on the author's property.

States like Wisconsin, Illinois, Iowa and to a lesser degree Minnesota have been putting out record deer for a long time. Large, heavy-bodied deer are the order of the day and the rolling timber/acorn country in the north and the more agricultural land in the south ensures there are enough nutrients to grow heavy racks. Through voluntary QDM and well managed state programs such as Earn-A-Buck (a state mandated increased doe harvest program) plus good genetics some real magnum deer are coming out of the Upper Midwest. Specifically look toward record producing counties such a Pike County, Illinois, Lacrosse and Buffalo County, Wisconsin as well as the coveted draw tags in Iowa as some of your top picks in this overall great region.

THE MIDWEST

The Midwest, while not as consistent at producing oversized deer as the Upper Midwest, still puts out some great bucks every year. States such as Missouri, Indiana, Kansas, Oklahoma and Ohio all have had some great deer hunting opportunities for big bucks. While more agricultural than the Upper Midwest the mix of crops (mainly corn) and wooded cover are ideal habitat for growing trophy racks that survive long enough to be classed record animals. As QDM grows in popularity, these states will start seeing bigger deer and provide even more opportunities. Of all the states Kansas has my vote for the best trophy whitetail hunting found in the Midwest of not in the nation.

THE GREAT PLAINS STATES

Until recently the Great Plains states were not really thought of for large whitetails as they were more often associated with fringe mule deer and antelope habitat, but as whitetails have expanded their range and adapted to the brush choked river drainages of the "near west" some monster deer have developed. In places like the Platte river of Nebraska, Wyoming and Colorado, the Missouri River in North and South Dakota, the numerous dry creeks in eastern Colorado and the infamous Milk River in Montana trophy class whitetails are thriving. I have seen more than one 200 inch deer come out of these zones or found their sheds. The reason for this is simple, there is ample cover, plenty of food and for the most part very little pressure. Traditionally speaking, whitetail are not the primary focus for residents or visiting hunters, in these states mule deer are much more of a draw. As mule deer opportunities are getting tougher all across the West (and becoming even more sought after) I don't see a

The South is not a sleeper anymore for monstrous whitetails, huge bucks like this one from Kentucky are becoming more of a reality. *Photo courtesy of Bill Miller.*

time in the near future when hunters in these states will start actively pursuing whitetails on a large scale – so for the immediate future at least the Great Plains states will still provide excellent whitetail hunting for trophy class animals.

THE SOUTH

The South has long been known for tremendous numbers of whitetail deer but not huge racked deer. That has all changed with QDM, food plots, and mineral supplements. Now more than ever big deer are coming out of the southern states. While filming a TV show for North American Hunter last season, my friend Bill Miller shot a 180 class deer in Kentucky. On a free range Texas hunt I have had several clients kill deer between 150 and 170 inches. There is no secret to growing trophy whitetails. Manage the herd, make sure they have everything they need in terms of food, water and cover and give them time to grow up and quality deer can be the result.

THE EAST

The East is the proverbial home of the whitetail. And there are more whitetails and consequently whitetail hunters in the eastern states than almost the rest of the country combined. This is especially true if you exclude the Upper Midwest, which has a large whitetail hunting following. Most of the eastern states are known for quantity not quality. Most deer get shot young and do not reach their full potential and since this has been the norm for many generations, it is doubtful if they have as good of genetics as other parts of the country. While there can be lots of opportunity in the East and certainly some great bucks come out of eastern sleeper pockets every year, hunters looking to harvest a trophy animal will do better to spend their time in other parts of the country.

WESTERN WHITETAIL

Contrary to popular belief Whitetails don't die when crossing the Rocky Mountains – they can and do survive and in some cases can grow to monstrous proportions. However, most people don't travel out West to, nor do many western locals, hunt whitetails. If people are going to travel that far they want something different like mule deer, elk, blacktail deer or even antelope. If you are looking for a unique trophy whitetail hunt, start looking around the northern panhandle of Idaho and the northeast corner of Washington State. Not only are there whitetail in the dense evergreen forests and steep mountains, but good ones at that. This is a real sleeper area that very few hunt, but more should, as there is a very good chance at bagging a record book animal.

Hot Spots: Buffalo County WI, Pike County Il, Milk River, MT
Best Season: November 1 -16 through much of their northern range for peak rut activity
Draw Odds: Most states have over the counter tags, but with certain trophy producing states like Kansas, Illinois and Iowa you will have to apply.
Sleeper Spots: northern Idaho and eastern Colorado
Cost: While guided whitetail hunts can cost a fortune, they can be hunted in almost any state on public land for the cost of the tag. Transportation to the spot, a cheap motel or tent camp and a tag and you could frugally do almost any of these hunts for $500 - $700.
World Record: 213 5/8 typical, 333 7/8 non-typical

MULE DEER

Next to elk, mule deer (Odocoileus Hemionus) are probably the most dreamed of species on a North American traveling hunter's wish list. Their racks grow tall and wide, the country they inhabit is still large, rugged and for the most part sparsely inhabited. Their pogo sticking gate, and their gray ghost-like coat intrigues hunters from coast to coast. But unlike whitetail that have expanded their range as well as their trophy size mule deer have not. Mule deer have suffered through some tough times. Their decrease has been due to a multitude of reasons; a changing landscape with an increased human population, various changing agricultural practices, increased whitetail encroachment and I personally believe a susceptibility to modern hunting techniques.

Whitetails can live and thrive in a small woodlot, maybe going undetected from area hunters for years. This is rarely the case with mule deer. In more open terrain a big buck gets discovered pretty

Mule deer are making a slow come back through many parts of the West. The author captured this beautiful buck on film a week before the season while scouting in Colorado, he was never seen again.

quickly by area hunters and their very nature of running for a hundred yards or so before turning around to take a final look at their pursuers often means a short life when hunters are armed with modern centerfire rifles.

It is not all doom and gloom for mule deer or hunters wishing to secure a trophy class animal. There are some magnificent animals in places across the West that are so physically hard to access, or are kept to an extremely limited entry either through the controls of a well managed ranch or a very limited state draw. And while many Boone and Crockett mule deer are taken each year I still feel this is one of North America's toughest animals to get into the record book. I have hunted mule deer since about the time I could hunt and they have been a lifelong passion for me. I have hunted some of the best trophy producing states for them under a variety of conditions with a multitude of weapons and while I have shot some great animals that I proudly consider personal trophies, none come close to the Boone and Crockett minimums. But all the scoring aside, any mule deer hunt is a great experience and every state has its own unique set of opportunities and challenges.

TROPHY STATES

If you want only one mule deer and are willing to wait for the best tag apply for the hardest to draw units in various western states combined with a late season (if they are hard to draw there is usually a reason – they produce good bucks). Southern Idaho, northern Arizona, parts of New Mexico, Utah, Colorado and Wyoming all can and do produce fantastic mule deer. Keep in mind drawing a tag will take anywhere from three years to a decade.

EASY TO ACCESS STATES

If you don't have the patience to wait for years to hunt a trophy state and would be just as pleased with a solid, 24 inch wide 150 class buck, there are states that can be hunted every year. Here are two great states known for their easy access and availability of over the counter tags.

WASHINGTON

When most hunters think of Washington State they think of blacktail deer, cougars, Roosevelt elk and black bears in the rain soaked western half of the state. Few think of the eastern half of the state that is comprised of dry land wheat fields, basalt canyons

Mule deer are tough to get in the record book. The author has taken several bucks of this caliber and while they will not come close to making any book, they are trophies of the West none-the-less.

and sagebrush flats that are home to a whole host of desert species including mule deer. From the Canadian border on the north to the Oregon border on the south, the eastern half of Washington has lots of good mule deer hunting. Managed more for quantity than quality most mature bucks are pretty average in terms of trophy quality, but occasionally a sleeper trophy does come out of Washington. What makes Washington attractive to the non-resident hunter is an abundance of over-the-counter tags for archery, muzzleloader as well as modern rifle. The state is broken up in a series of very small units, which makes understanding the regulations a difficult proposition for hunters not familiar with the country. For drawing a coveted limited entry tag into a trophy unit, Washington seriously drops the ball. Residents and nonresidents alike are forced to buy their hunting license/deer tag for a specific weapon (archery, muzzleloader or rifle) then apply for a draw unit. If the hunter is unsuccessful applying for the draw (which the majority of the time they are) they are stuck with the original tag they bought. No refunds, no changing weapons, etc. For the hunter traveling to Washington for the first time I would select a unit that has lots of public ground and would hunt a primitive season (archery or muzzleloader) to avoid the crowds.

NEBRASKA

Nebraska is a great state for mule deer. Not known for huge trophy potential, Nebraska does have several other things going for it. It has readily available over-the-counter tags in many prime regions for rifle, muzzleloader and archery. Some regions also have a good concentration of mule deer despite a CWD outbreak/scare in the early 2000's. The downside to Nebraska is the serious lack of public land across the state. Most of this state is comprised of large private ranches. Still, depending on where you are in the state, hunters can get lots of good access simply for the asking. The key is having an up-to-date Platt map and local phone book to determine ownership. Most Nebraska ranches are large sprawling affairs that often make determining ownership difficult. Once ownership is discovered, I have had pretty good luck in getting permission to hunt. While there is not a lot of public land, what's available is pretty large solitary chunks that have some great opportunities. For mule deer look toward the central portion of the state most notably around the Valentine National Wildlife refuge and the far north western

Mule deer of this caliber are generally only found, with any consistency, on private land or on public land that is well managed for trophy potential through limited access.

corner of the state in the Pine Ridge National Forest and the Ogallala Grassland. Between these three spots public land hunters have access to thousands of acres of prime mule deer habitat. Luckily for hunters willing to put in the effort, the road access in all of these areas is not overabundant which reduces the pressure on some large sections of country. While all public access hunting areas receive the most pressure around the roads, it has been my experience that in Nebraska this is even more pronounced. The locals have a very ingrained "road hunting" culture and with laws that allow loaded, uncased firearms within a vehicle further encourage this behavior. While road hunting is abhorrent it does mean good things for hunters willing to work. Get away from a public road by as a little as a mile and the amount of game you see goes up dramatically.

Hot Spots: Colorado, Nevada, Utah and Arizona for good trophies Nebraska, and Washington for hunting ease

Best Season: Late November for a prime rut hunt

Draw Odds: Most really good rifle mule deer hunting is by draw and the odds range from around 10% success to single digits. Without getting a landowner tag or hunting with a primitive weapon you will apply for along time

Sleeper Spots: Nebraska, South Dakota and North Dakota. Nebraska is good because it is over the counter, South Dakota and North Dakota require a draw but have really good odds with better than average bucks.

Cost: Mule deer are quickly becoming the most expensive guided western species, sometimes even surpassing elk. That being said, if you can get a tag or choose to hunt an over-the-counter state you can do the hunt pretty affordably. Consider $1,200 an average do it yourself mule deer hunt.

World Record: 226 4/8 typical, 355 2/8 non-typical

Blacktail Deer

Of all of the deer species available to hunters, those who have hunted blacktail deer, especially the Columbia variety, generally agree they are the toughest of all the deer subspecies to hunt. Originally thought of as a sub-species of mule deer, more recent studies suggest it was early breading of whitetail does and blacktail bucks that created mule deer, not the other way around as so commonly believed.

At any rate, whatever their lineage, the results were an innate wariness, a nearly complete nocturnal behavior (for mature bucks)

and a home that is as impenetrable as any jungle in the world. Add all these factors up and it is easy to see why hanging your tag on a trophy blacktail can be such a chore.

Columbia blacktail deer extend from central British Columbia south through Washington State, Oregon and into California at Monterey bay. Their east to west boundaries extend roughly from the Pacific Coast to the top of the Cascade Mountain range. Growing up on the western slope of Washington's Cascade Range I cut my deer hunting teeth on blacktail. It is some of the most frustrating, toughest, hardest hunting I have ever done and after years of doing it my best trophy is a 3 x 3 that would score about half of the minimum entry for any record book. I still look at that buck's rack hanging on the wall with admiration and satisfaction every time I see it. Blacktail deer taught me a lot about hunting.

Columbia blacktails like this one with Author's long time hunting partner Taro Sakita, are hard to find. With patience, the right tactics and hunting the right season they can be pulled out of the rain-soaked Pacific Northwest jungle. Unfortunately, the author has never done as well. *Photo courtesy of Taro Sakita*

Most people after their first experience hunting blacktails think they are doing something wrong, are hunting the wrong area or just are there at the wrong time of the year. This is generally not the case. Blacktails are just elusive. Their home range is nearly identical over its entire area so there is no reason for them to move with the season (there are some limited exceptions to this, but for the most part their range stays the same year around). Since they are browsers by nature, they are constantly surrounded by food. Since it rains nearly every day during the season they can literally stay in the thickest bedding area they choose, and feed and drink without moving more than 10 yards. When going after blacktails you have the odds stacked against you, but before prospective blacktail hunters everywhere throw up their collective arms in surrender, there are a few tricks and techniques I did pick up over the dozen or so years I spent getting bettered by them that definitely increase a hunter's chances.

THE RIGHT TIME

As I previously stated, blacktails don't move very much and when they do, if they have any antlers at all it is generally under the cover of darkness. The one exception to this rule is during the rut. Unlike the whitetail rut, which is very well researched, documented and patterned, local western hunters pay very little attention to the blacktail rut. While it is not nearly as pronounced as the whitetail rut it still happens and can create some fantastic opportunities. You won't see many scrapes or rubs, you will find a few, but more importantly you will see a vastly increased deer movement, especially of bucks, during daylight hours. It takes place anytime from mid to late November. Whitetail scents and traditional rattling, while almost unused by local hunters, can and will work – I have personally seen both techniques succeed.

THE RIGHT FOOD

Since blacktails are primarily browsers constantly surrounded by their food of choice patterning a food source is next to impossible. They rarely come out into open fields to eat crops and I have yet to see a traditional planted food plot raise nary a blacktail eyebrow, however there are a couple of things they do like and will travel for. Young clover is one. If you can find a source of sweet clover (either through a planted food plot patch or along side of an area where it was planted to control erosion, very common on logging roads and building projects) you will catch blacktails eating it. The next most appealing food to blacktails is apples. The Pacific Northwest has an abundance of old, overgrown and long abandoned apple orchards left over from old farms and homesteads. In the fall when the apples start to drop they generally won't make it through the night before blacktails eat them. By staking out either of these food sources early in the morning or late in the evening you can increase you chances of success dramatically.

WASHINGTON

Of the three states that have blacktails Washington is probably the poorest bet for the visiting hunting. While there is lots of public land, finding quality game is a problem. Blacktails are reclusive and hard to hunt by their sheer nature, but finding trophy bucks in Washington State is extremely difficult. Much of this problem is due to urban sprawl and loss of prime habitat. If hunters must hunt Washington for blacktails look toward the Olympic Peninsula for the best mix of public land, trophy potential and overall deer density.

OREGON

Oregon is a far better bet for the visiting sportsman. The entire western slope of the Cascade Mountain range in Oregon to the coast is prime blacktail habitat and there is an abundance of public ground as well as large tracts of private ground traditionally open for public access. For those concerned with trophy book records look to southern Oregon, especially the Applegate unit, where hunters have an excellent chance at tagging a trophy blacktail.

CALIFORNIA

Northern California is home to some huge blacktails, but it is not my first choice for a visiting hunter. To begin with the best hunting generally comes on private land, and this is not free for the asking in California. Most prime California blacktail spots are on large ranches with guided programs in place. Next to the private land issue, blacktail hunting in California is more akin to mule deer hunting – not that there isn't anything wrong with that, but I just feel you miss part of the experience that is blacktail hunting. In my humble Pacific-Northwest-Rainforest opinion, a true blacktail hunt is not complete without battling some of what the traditional Pacific Northwest has to offer – daily bone-soaking downpours, old growth cedar trees, sasquatch-sized ferns, hanging moss, devils clubs and the infamous banana slugs. For a true blacktail hunter missing all of this is like owning a dog without ears.

Sitka Blacktails

The blacktails talked about thus far have been of the Columbia variety; the other species is the Sitka blacktail primarily found on the Alaskan Islands. The Sitka is vastly more common to hunt and in many cases makes the basis for the most affordable of all Alaskan hunting experiences. Classified as an animal in Alaska that a guide is not required to hunt. Many nonresident hunters head north to experience this unique state while doing an unguided blacktail hunt. With liberal limits, high success rates and lots of public land to roam, this is an ideal hunt for sportsman looking to experience some exotic hunting on a budget.

While guided hunts are available, most hunters choose to do it themselves. There are several options for doing it yourself. In some instances hunters will reserve a USFS cabin (there are many of these cabins throughout southeast Alaska, see the resource section of this book for more details) for a week's hunt. These cabins provide a wonderful experience. Snug, dry and warm, but not fancy, they provide one of the best camps a hunter will ever experience and best of all are extremely inexpensive. In some cases you can drive right to them, but in most others you have to charter a small plane or take a boat. Another option for traveling hunters is somewhere between buying a guided hunt and completely doing it yourself. It is generally called "hunting with a licensed transporter".

In Alaska there are guides and transporters. Transporters can, as their name implies, transport you to and from an area, but not actually guide you to a species. Most transporters specializing in blacktails however do a bit more than simply transport you to and from the area. They generally have a place for you to stay (some use large live-aboard boats, other have land based cabins), some provide food and supplies, and most can help you facilitate the logistics of your hunt. As imagined these services cost about half of a guided hunt and are a great deal for first timers to Alaska who want the experience without trying it all alone.

Hot Spots: Southern Oregon for Columbian Blacktail, Kodiak Island Alaska for Sitka blacktail

Best Season: Hunt mid to late November through much of their range to hit peak rut activity

Draw Odds: All states with blacktails offer over the counter tags, however look for special hunts in parks and limited entry draw areas for trophy potential

Sleeper Spots: Almost all blacktails spots are sleeper hunts, outside the Pacific Northwest few hunters have tried for them.

Blacktails don't get the massive racks of their whitetail or mule deer cousins, so this buck is a true trophy animal. Blacktails are a challenging hunt and not for the meek. Be prepared and you too can enjoy hunting these magnificent animals.

Best Value Hunt: Either a do it yourself hunt in Oregon or for a first time Alaska experience head to Kodiak Island.

Cost: A good hunt to Oregon could be put together for under a $1,000. Alaska would cost roughly double as getting there is one of the biggest expenses.

World Record: Columbia blacktail 182 2/8 typical, 208 1/8 non-typical, Sitka blacktail 133 typical, 134 non-typical

ELK

For most prospective elk hunters, the thought of an elk hunt means one thing; Rocky Mountain elk in the heart of the Rocky Mountains specifically Montana, Idaho or Wyoming. While this is well and good there is a lot more to elk and elk hunting than this relatively small patch of terra firma. Elk are now spread through the United States and have stable, huntable populations for non-residents from the west coast to the eastern plains of Colorado and from the northern border of the US nearly down to Mexico. In addition to traveling west, many eastern resident hunters are getting a crack at elk in their home state. With rehabilitated herds across the United States there is no better time than the present to go after the magnificent wapiti. And with this broadening of locales, non-resident hunters should also think about broadening species. In addition to Rocky Mountain elk, Roosevelt elk of the Pacific Northwest provide some of the best do-it-yourself opportunities found today.

Roosevelt Elk

My first elk hunting experience was for Roosevelt elk. At the time I didn't appreciate them for what they are. Little did I know that thousands of hunters across the West who had shot dozens of Rocky Mountain elk apiece would give their soul to harvest a single good Roosevelt. To my youthful ignorance I saw Rosies as a large bodied, but diminutively racked sub-species of the more "majestic" Rocky Mountain elk. How wrong I was. But luckily it only took me 20 some years to realize this. Now each year regardless of where I am elk

Alaskan Mike Wheat poses with a trophy buck taken on a do-it-yourself hunt on Kodiak.

Hunting elk in the rut is something every hunter should experience once in their life. Nothing compares to hearing their shrill bugle echo out of a dark timber canyon.

hunting I think back to those times in the old growth cedar swamps, listening to the shrill bugle of a love sick bull looking for a harem. In the early morning fog that is so prevalent along the Pacific Coast watching their nearly white bodies drift in and out of the mist is a sight that all hunters should behold once in their hunting career – thankfully I did.

For hunters looking for a completely unique hunt, nothing quite compares to Roosevelt elk. The largest bodied of the three elk species, Roosevelt elk are found in Washington, Oregon, British Columbia and on a limited basis, Alaska. Of all their locations, the most cost effective and feasible locations to hunt them are Washington and Oregon west of Interstate 5. Both states offer over-the-counter licenses. The cover the elk are found in remains pretty consistent regardless of where they are hunted. Stands of swamp cedar in the Pacific Northwest rainforest is their preferred habitat, but they can also be found in good numbers in agricultural settings as well as clear cuts that have several years of regrowth on them. When it comes to finding a bargain trophy outside of British Columbia which is very expensive the two best places today is the far western Olympic peninsula and in the far northwest corner of Oregon namely the Wilson and Trask units

Archery hunters really have an advantage in these two states as their season offers the closest time to hunt them in the rut. Since the cover is so dense getting close is not as difficult as many imagine, the biggest challenge is keeping dry as well as following a blood trail in wet weather. In this part of the world over 100 inches of rain annually is not uncommon so be prepared to hunt in wet weather.

Do-it-yourself Roosevelt hunts are almost the only way to hunt them as so few people outside of British Columbia are offering guided or private land hunts. I would suppose the main reason for this is due to the country they inhabit. The core region of the Roosevelt's range is public land generally in the form of National Forest. This makes outfitting hard as it can be so unpredictable. This can spell success for do-it-yourself hunters. Study some topo maps of the region, pick your season and head out with a pack strapped on. Plan on hiking as far away from other hunters as you can and with enough work you will surely encounter elk, and even if not you will have a wonderful time on one of the last great rainforests of North America.

Rocky Mountain Elk

Rocky Mountain elk are quite possibly the big game animal most often sought by traveling American hunters. From Pennsylvania to Florida whitetail deer hunters dream of one day getting the chance

Hunting Roosevelt elk is a very unique experience very few get to enjoy. They inhabit the dark, wet rainforests of the Pacific Northwest. If hunters go after them with bow or muzzleloader they can still experience them in the rut.

to hunt the magnificent wapiti. The story of the American elk is an amazing recovery tale and they are now found in states that have not seen them in the last 100 years (many of which offer extremely limited resident only hunting seasons) the main opportunity to hunt them still lies in the West. Since there is so much public land across the West this is still a hunt that can be done by anyone if they have the motivation.

However, keep in mind if your definition of "success" is to harvest an animal and you will not be satisfied until you do, then doing it yourself over the long run may not be your cheapest bet. When considering the fact that the overall odds of hanging your tag on a bull (any bull) on an unguided public land hunt will take several years to accomplish, you may be money ahead keeping an eye open for a quality private land hunt at a bargain price.

That being said, if you measure "success" in terms of getting the privilege to just experience the high country, see elk and listen to them bugle and consider actually shooting one just a bonus then there is little reason why you can't do this hunt on your own. Even if you don't get one it is still an incredible hunt

In terms of dollars and sense, the "on foot" variety of elk hunt is the best bet. You can drive to many western regions where hundreds

The author and hunting partner with a very respectable do-it-yourself bull.

Nothing is more inspiring to hear on a hunt than the scream of a bugling bull elk. Once you have him calling and coming toward you, the game is in full swing.

of miles of land are available for the walking. Park your pickup where the road ends, load up a pack with the right gear and take off. Essentially this hunt costs whatever the tag price is, the cost of fuel to get to your destination, some minimal groceries (which you would eat at home anyway) and some hunting gear. Your odds for success will be less than 20%, but the chance of having a good time will be nearly guaranteed.

The next step in terms of perceived quality versus expense is the horse back drop camp hunt. Personally I don't really like drop camps using a horse pack string for several reasons. To begin with, hiring a pack string is not as cheap as many people would have you believe, secondly they generally have set trail systems they work, (to make any money a packer has to run many trips, which means most hunters are getting dumped in the same neck of the woods) and finally you are generally held to someone else's schedule. This means you usually won't be picked up until the predetermined time. While this may be ok if you tag out early (rarely occurs, but can happens), a more likely situation is your group is not seeing any game and wants to move, but are stuck until the pack string comes back. The upside is you can often stay as long as you like (within reason) without incurring any extra charges, they allow you to have a much more comfortable, well-stocked camp and means you can hunt farther from the road and still recover game. Sometimes horse back hunts work great; sometimes they are less than satisfying. It really depends upon the packer and your needs to determine if this kind of hunt will work for you.

Close to the Road Bulls

One of the biggest mistakes many first time elk hunters make is overlooking honey holes because they think they are "too close to civilization." Elk will often adapt like whitetails and literally be living in good numbers within a couple miles of a western town's city limit sign. The most common trait visiting hunters do is look at a map, pick a spot that is the most remote and head in. I had some friends plan a Colorado elk hunt a number of years ago. They had their own horses and poured over maps of their unit trying to find a likely looking bowl far away from a trailhead. Finally they found one that was about 15 miles away from any road. The week of the hunt they headed out and drove to Colorado, unloaded their horses, packed them up and headed in. It took them a full day to get to their proposed camping spot and when they crested the final ridgeback they were faced with the stuff that dreams are made of: an open high alpine meadow with short grass, an elk wallow on one side and a small babbling brook running through its center – Shangri-La for elk hunters. Oh yeah, I almost forgot to mention the 14 other groups camped in the same meadow, making it appear to be a camo clad Woodstock in the mountains. After a week of hunting they saddled up, sans any elk, and headed home. Just because a place is remote doesn't mean it will be devoid of pressure or full of elk. On that same vein, some of the biggest bulls I have ever shot were within sight of the ranch house and one was less than ½ mile from a major highway. Elk are where you find them. Don't be fooled into thinking you always have to get deep into the backcountry to have success.

Hot Spots: My personal favorite hotspot for Roosevelt elk is on the northern part of the Olympic Peninsula of Washington. For Rocky Mountain elk, Wyoming, southern Colorado, New Mexico and Arizona all are fantastic

Best Season: Any season that falls from mid-September into early October. This usually is an archery or muzzleloader season.

Sleeper Spots: Northeast corner of Oregon for Rocky Mountain elk - rough country and limited access but good bulls.

Best Value Hunt: Colorado wins the value hunt award as it is easy to access for most eastern hunters driving or flying, there is lots of public land and lots of elk. Success is good on small to medium size bulls. For Roosevelt elk Washington's price for their over the counter elk tag is a bargain (same price as their deer tag) and there is lots of public land within a few hour drive of Seattle.

Cost: A bare bones do it yourself tent camp for elk can still be done for $1,000. It will be cutting it close and may need several buddies chipping in for fuel, but it can be done.

World Record: Roosevelt elk 404 6/8 typical, Rocky Mountain 442 5/8 typical, 465 2/8 non-typical

MOOSE

Moose are the quintessential animal of the North, and is a must have for many big game hunters. Unfortunately it is not an easily affordable animal to hunt throughout much of its range. In Canada for the most part a guide is required, which puts it out of the realm for many, but good deals can still be had on guided archery hunts in many Canadian provinces as well as some fantastic deals on last minute cancellation rifle hunts. Next to archery tags and cancellation hunts, the province of Newfoundland is quite possibly the best buy on moose today for a guided hunt. The moose in Newfoundland are considered Eastern Canadian moose and can tip the scales at over 1,000 pounds with almost a 60 inch spread on the rack. There are many very good outfitters in Newfoundland and the country has an extremely high population of moose making the success rate nearly 100%. While the trophy potential is not great, for hunters looking to experience moose hunting at its finest, get lots of action and bring home some great meat, Newfoundland is hard to beat.

By far and large doing a moose hunt on your own is the most inexpensive way to hunt them, but as anyone who has done this can attest to, you pay for it one way or another and on an unguided hunt you pay for it in terms of blood, sweat and tears.

One of the best aspects of a guided hunt for moose is not so much the actual guiding (don't underestimate the value of this either), but it is the physical labor and equipment to help make the job easier after the trigger is pulled. The average hunter has no idea how big a moose is until they walk up on their first dead one. They just keep growing and growing with every step. A good outfitter will have either horses, ATVs, boats or some other means of getting a moose out

Moose are enormous when alive, but after you've made the kill and get close to one, you can really see the massiveness of these wonderful creatures. One tip for the moose hunter is to take several sharp knives and a sharpener with you. Field dressing a moose is an all day affair.

of the backcountry. If you do it yourself, you will need to think of this and plan accordingly ahead of time. For destinations where hunters can go unguided, Maine and Vermont come to mind as the easiest of all lower 48 states to draw a tag. Both are draw states, but are open to nonresidents and the odds are not unrealistically bad – if a hunter diligently applies there is a decent chance of drawing a tag sometime

Ray Howell, noted international bowhunter and founder of Kicking Bear not only made his big game dreams come true, but helps thousands of kids each year fulfill their own hunting dreams.

Amber Wheat of Alaska posing with her second-ever bow kill. This huge 62" moose is a dream trophy for anyone and is a great example of a trophy animal taken on a budget.

Bull moose have the power to fling a fully grown grizzly bear like a rag doll, so imagine the force expended when two bulls lock antlers in battle. Wherever you hunt moose, you are sure to have an adventure.

in the next 10 to 20 years. Both have a good access to where the moose live and do have outfitters that can help with equipment to get the moose out at a reasonable cost.

Next on the lower 48 list is the Shiras or Wyoming moose. Found throughout the Rocky Mountains the Shiras is the smallest of the North American moose species. They typically max out in terms of weight around 1,000 for a large bull and have a rack that spreads 40-50 inches wide. Nonresidents can apply for tags in Wyoming, Montana, Idaho, Washington, and Utah. The draw odds range from really bad to not so bad, but nowhere within its range can a draw for Shiras be deemed as good.

The final option and quite possibly the ultimate test for the tried and true do-it-yourselfer is an Alaskan wilderness unguided hunt for the gigantic Alaskan-Yukon strain of moose. Until one of these behemoths is seen up close most hunters don't realize their enormous size. Capable of tipping the scales at over 1,500 pounds on the hoof with a rack that spreads into the 70 inch range, which can weigh an equal number of pounds this one heck of a lot of weight to get out of the woods.

In short this is a hunt for the extremely fit, young or dumb. If you fit into any of these categories read on, if not skip to the next section.

Moose hunting in Alaska by yourself or with a few good friends sounds like a great idea at the time, but those who have done it know it is an awful lot of work. The country where the bulls live is tough to negotiate alone, let alone with a load of moose meat. It can be very dangerous and is often inhabited by large grizzly or brown bears you have to deal with, who coincidently like to eat moose meat. Camping takes on an entirely new meaning in the Alaskan wilderness. No keeping food or meat in camp, cook outside of your tent and sleep with a firearm – a bit like the KOA outside of Detroit.

But if you must do it once in your life and many of us have to, I recommend organizing a float hunt. While no method of hunting moose by yourself in Alaska is easy this may be the easiest a non-guided, non-resident can achieve. There are several transportation services that will drop you into a river system with a whitewater raft and allow you to float to a predetermined pick up point down stream. This way you can float and hunt, get out in likely looking areas and hunt within a few hundred yards to a half a mile away from the river. Hopefully you will encounter a bull along the river, even better if he stays there after the shot.

Hot Spots: Newfoundland, and Alaska

Best Season: Generally there isn't much latitude in moose seasons. Almost all across their range they are hunted in early October. Some good deal archery hunts can take place in September.

Sleeper Hunts: Newfoundland guided hunts are a great buy, as are Ontario and Saskatchewan archery hunts and hunters have been recently killing some great animals in both provinces.

Best Value Hunt: By far and large the best price hunt for a moose in sheer dollars and sense is a do-it-yourself trip to Alaska. You will pay for it in other ways than cash though and may opt to spend the money and save your back and hunt them in Newfoundland.

Cost: Ontario guided rifle hunts sell for between $5,000 and $6,500, last minute deals and archery hunts may be had for half. Newfoundland can be hunted for $4,000 as can Alaska on a completely do-it-yourself trip

World Record: Alaska-Yukon 261 5/8, Canada 242, Shiras 205 4/8

SHEEP

It is hard to list sheep in a book of bargain big game trips, as sheep around the world are typically not thought of as inexpensive animals. It is shocking for a hunter new to the sport of big game hunting to find out that traveling to Africa, South America, New Zealand or nearly any place else is the world is vastly cheaper than hunting our own indigenous North American sheep species. Rough taxonomy breaks the North American sheep into two main categories; bighorn sheep and thin horn sheep. Of the bighorn sheep there are Rocky Mountain bighorn, California bighorn, and Desert bighorn. The North American thin horn sheep include the Dall's and Stone's sheep. Of the sheep discussed in this book I am going to keep it to Rocky Mountain, California and desert bighorn sheep as they are the only ones that hunters on a budget can ever afford to be able to hunt (Dall's and

Few hunters realize that sheep hunting can be affordable, if a tag is drawn.

While Dall's sheep are not a Do-It-Yourself trip, for non-residents of Alaska, if hunters can find a reasonably priced guided hunt, Dall's can be the most inexpensive guided sheep hunt around. At the time of this writing, Dall's don't cost much more than a guided western elk hunt. *Photo courtesy of Mike Lunenschloss.*

Stone's require a guide for non-residents making them out of the reach of most budgets).

For the three previously mentioned species there are essentially about three ways to get a tag – through a state draw, raffle or auction. If and when a tag for these species can be purchased through an auction the laws of supply and demand quickly push them out of the realm of possibility for the average person. Most states that allow hunting them generally have a very limited amount of tags outside of the draw that are either raffled or auctioned off. The money raised by both activities go back to sheep research, habitat improvement and rehabilitation work as sheep are very susceptible to loss of habitat and even more so to diseases brought in from domestic livestock. Of the three methods of getting a tag the auction is simply not feasibly in a book on budget hunting as the tags regularly sell for $50,000 to over $100,000 each – making them out of reach to all but the ultra-wealthy.

Depending upon the state or organization a raffle may or may not be something you want to participate in. The odd of securing a sheep tag through a raffle are long at best and when the cost of the raffle is added up compounded with the normal time it could take to actually win (based on odds), you will spend a considerable amount of money. For example, if by buying enough tickets to get the odds down to around 1 chance in 50 a hunter will probably spend about $200. Multiply that $200 by the 50 years it should take to draw a tag and it is easy to see that the tag alone for this hunt will cost about $10,000 and by the time you win you will more than likely be too old to actually go on the hunt. We all like to think we are lucky and will win by buying a ticket. The odds are just not with you. However if you like donating money to a good cause to support wildlife this is an excellent way to do it and who knows, you might actually win a tag someday.

Now that auctions and raffles are covered, let discuss more realistic means of securing a sheep tag, which is the general state draw. Of states that have sheep species Washington, Oregon, California, New Mexico, Arizona, Utah, Nevada, Idaho, Montana, Colorado and Wyoming have draws open to non-residents. All of these states have unique rules and requirements for their draws and depending upon how they conduct the draw (some require a license to be bought to participate, some charge the money for the license fee up front, some may allow you to purchase bonus points, etc) the odds range anywhere from 1 in 1,000 to as low as 1 in 10. While this doesn't sound very good at first, it is not that bad. By entering these draws

If you ever get the opportunity to hunt any of North America's wild sheep, you will find a life-changing experience that few ever get to share. For many hunters, sheep hunts are at the apex of their dream lists.

every year your odds may go up (depending upon their preference system) and if you do it for all of the states you can afford you even better your odds. By heavily applying for state draws every hunter stands a realistic chance of drawing a least one sheep tag somewhere in his or her lifetime if they stick with it.

The final method for harvesting a Rocky Mountain bighorn is buying an unlimited tag. At the time of this writing, Montana still has a few units that are unlimited sheep units. When told this for this first time most hunters are shocked. "I thought sheep tags were hard to get, and harvest strictly controlled, how can they have unlimited sheep tags." Well there is a catch. To begin with the unlimited unit has to be your first and only choice when filling out your application. This means that you cannot apply for a coveted high success draw tag unit, fail to draw and then put in for an unlimited unit. You have to apply only for an unlimited unit from the start. Second catch is the unit is subject to closure within a 48 hour notice. Finally the unit is controlled as to how many sheep can be taken. The number is generally low (two or three) and when those animals are taken the unit is closed, with no refunds given for hunters who may not have even gotten in the field yet – and it is the hunter's responsibility in the field to check with the Department of Fish and Wildlife to know about closures. To top this all off, the units themselves are extremely rugged and hard to access. Hiking in by foot and packing all your gear in and out (including your sheep within 48 hours of harvest) pretty much self regulates this hunts. But even so, for hunters with a passion to hunt sheep, but not the financial means this is the last of the cheap, do-able sheep hunts in the world.

Hot Spots: Idaho is probably the best state for drawing tags in, but will also cost the most to apply.

Draw Odds: Draw odds range from as low as 1 in 8 to 1 in a 1,000 applicants

Sleeper Spots: Probably the biggest sleeper spot is the Montana unlimited tag hunt in south central Montana. This hut is also the best value sheep hunt. For a little over $800 in tags and licenses hunters can be pursuing sheep next season with an over-the-counter tag. However there is a catch. Smaller sheep, very few sheep, low success rate and impossibly rugged country to access – oh yeah I almost forgot as soon as the quota is taken the unit is closed with no refunds. A great price, but not necessarily a great hunt.

Best Value Hunt: Cancellation Alaskan guided Dall's sheep hunts may be the best value. Good success rates, great scenery, low tag price and no draw and if seriously price-shopped on a last minute cancellation hunt can be found way south of $10,000.

Cost: Bargain sheep hunts range from ultra low $2,000 DIY trips to Montana to $10,000 bargain Dall's hunts. Like all species the sky is the limit on what can be paid.

World Record: Rocky Mountain bighorn 208 3/8, desert 205 1/8

MOUNTAIN GOAT

Much of the information that has been written about sheep really also applies to mountain goat, just to a slightly lesser degree because the demand for them does not appear to be as high. For getting a tag in the lower 48 the method is exactly the same. Tags can be obtained through draw, raffle and auction just like sheep. Where goats differ a bit is that for hunters willing to travel with little notice somewhat decent deals can be had on guided cancellations hunts in Canada and southeast Alaska.

I will not try and convince someone that a good deal on a goat hunt is cheap. It is not. When compared to guided elk hunts in the Rockies, trophy mule deer trips and even trophy whitetails in Canada, goat prices are on par. If it is something that a hunter seriously wants, the

Hunters need to be in peak physical condition and be prepared down to every last detail if you plan to go after mountain goats. They are wary animals with excellent vision and they live in the most remote mountain areas to be found.

best option is probably to buy a last minute cancellation hunt tag.

The odds of drawing a tag in the lower 48 are slightly better than any of the sheep species. They are still long and when you compare the fees associated with drawing (over the course of time needed to draw), plus the actual tag cost if you draw, you will see that it quickly equals almost as much as if you just bought a "good deal" guided hunt. And, you still have to conduct the hunt yourself. This means getting your gear into the backcountry and providing all the food and supplies. This is one hunt that is very hard to do in the lower 48 on your own as inexpensively as hiring a guide in Alaska or Canada.

If you do decide to look for the best deal possible on a guided hunt right now Alaska seems to be a better buy than Canada. And for trophy goats it is hard to beat southeast Alaska, specifically the Misty Fjord region. It is a tough hunt for sure, but the long coats of the late season and the trophy horns make it a good hunt to do.

Hot Spots: Southeast Alaska, Idaho, and Montana

Best Season: Most hunters prefer later if given the choice. Longer hair, and lower elevations make the difference.

Draw Odds: This ranges from over the counter in Alaska (with a guide) to 1 in several hundred in some states.

Best Value Hunt: The best value is often found in state raffles. Better odds than the general draw at the same or lower application price and the winning ticket receives the tag for free.

Cost: If a tag is drawn a hunt could possibly be conducted for under $3,000. A good deal on an Alaskan guided hunt is around $6,000.

World Record: 56 6/8

Mountain goats often require miles of hiking, climbing and even crawling over loose rock that can make the trip very physically and mentally draining. But they sure are worth it. *Photo courtesy of Craig Boddington*

ANTELOPE

Antelope or pronghorn as they are also called are many hunters first experience with western game. And what a great first experience they make. They are plentiful, cover a large region, tags are easy to get and a hunt for them doesn't break the bank. I often recommend antelope to first time western hunters for just these reasons – not to mention success is generally very high.

Unlike other western big game species such as elk and mule deer that supply keeps going down (or at least access to the supply) and demand keeps going up, increasing the price to hunt them, antelope are pretty stable. They have a high population often spread over large tracts of public land making them quite accessible.

For the hunter looking to do a completely do-it-yourself hunt

One of the best western hunts for the do-it-yourself hunter is the pronghorn antelope. They offer an excellent challenge with vision equal to you with an 8X binocular. They also can show bursts of speed and a keen wariness for danger. Be ready for a long shot and lots of scouting. Also be ready for excellent table fare should you connect.

The author has hunted antelope in several western states, but likes eastern Colorado the best for numbers combined with trophy potential.

without the help of an outfitter, antelope are nearly ideal. As I stated, they are readily accessible on public land and to a large degree on private land. Ranchers who wouldn't think of letting you hunt other big game species, often welcome antelope hunters. The "speed goats" of the prairie have developed a bad reputation among ranchers for running through fences (I have personally witnessed this on several occasions). In addition to the broad access, antelope hunting really doesn't require a lot of specialized gear. A standard SUV or pick up truck is all that is needed to negotiate most of the West they call home and once an antelope is harvested, dealing with them is easy. If you can field dress a whitetail by yourself, you can easily field dress and load an antelope by yourself. For hunters flying to and from their hunting location, the animals can be quartered and the meat, cape and horns can be packed into one large cooler and sent home as checked baggage on the airline. If hunters needed another reason to hunt antelope, the tag for them is among the cheapest of all big game tags in the West, making it an affordable hunt for many.

I have hunted antelope in several western states, with rifle, muzzleloader and bow and have found all methods an exciting, and fulfilling challenge. Obviously antelope with their excellent eyesight were made for long range riflemen, and hunting them with a flat shooting rifle topped with a good scope is a relatively easy affair. There are many more opportunities for archery hunters and to a lesser degree muzzleloader hunters and the open range is far less crowded. When I first started antelope hunting with primitive weapons, I thought the proposition to be nearly impossible, but after spending some serious time chasing them around the plains I figured a few things out.

The first thing archery or muzzleloader hunters should get is a good quality portable blind. By employing a pop up blind beside a heavily used waterhole, and having the patience to sit there all day it is only a matter of time before a decent shot is presented. Next to sitting at a waterhole, hunting antelope in the rut (generally around the beginning of October through much of their range) is another good way of increasing your odds. Like almost all species in the rut, males let their guard down as well as become very aggressive when rounding up a harem of females. Using a decoy, hunters can sneak close, and often will draw an aggressive buck to them, looking for a fight. This hunt is not only affordable it is extremely exciting. If you are looking for a western species to break in on, look no further than antelope.

Hot Spots: Arizona, New Mexico, Montana and Wyoming

Best Season: The rut kits in between the end of Sept and early October through much of the antelopes range. Any season around these dates is stellar.

Draw Odds: Range from over the counter to low digit draw percentage.

Sleeper Spots: Nebraska and South Dakota

Best Value Hunt: Wyoming may be the best value. Lots of animals, an easy do it yourself hunt with high success.

Cost: This is a hunt that can literally be done for the tag fee and cost to get to the area. Camping is readily accessible as are sandwiches on the tailgate of the pickup. Very little special equipment is needed.

World Record: 95

COLLARED PECCARY (JAVELINA)

I shot my first javelina with a handgun down in south Texas. A troup, or I imagine more properly called a sounder, of them came snuffing and feeing down a arid, dusty trail. When they got to within 60 yards I cocked back the hammer of my Smith and Wesson and lined up the sights – the sight picture resembled a metallic silhouette range with banks of perfectly proportioned javelinas lined up in a

Javelinas make for a great winter diversion for the handgun hunters, archers or muzzleloading hunters. Wherever they are found, they are often an inexpensive hunt with liberal limits on game taken.

neat row. I squeezed off the shot and the rear javelina, the largest in the group, and he tipped over. It was rather anti-climatic, but what a rush. I figured out right then and there that in the future I wasn't going to spend all the cold winter days up in Wisconsin, next year I was heading back down south in search of more javelinas.

I am not alone in these sentiments – when old man winter blows his cold breath around the eaves of a houses buried in snow, many of the inhabitants, if they are hunters, have headed south for a little porker shooting in the sun. While not actually related to pigs javelinas provide fine winter sport. Fun to hunt, plenty of action and readily suitable for handguns, and archery equipment javelina hunting is a "must do" at least once.

Javelina are not listed by Boone and Crockett as a big game species, but Safari Club International classifies them and I personally consider them a big game animal. Native to the southwestern states, Mexico and into South America collared peccary are one of two sub species of peccary found in the Americas, the other being the white lipped

Pigs are a great example on non-indigenous species, overpopulating regions and consequently providing hunting opportunities. Many of which can be had for a free while Javelina hunting.

peccary of Central and South America. While not overly gifted in the sight department their sense of smell is excellent making them somewhat challenging to hunt.

After Christmas most hunters can't hardly think of spending the next nine month without something to hunt, and after the winter doldrums set in for good, it is often a great excuse to head south to warmer weather and hot hunting action.

In addition to javelinas, feral hogs inhabit much of the south and can be another exciting hunt often done at the exact same time and place. With year around seasons and bag limits pretty much non-existent, hog hunting can be another fun pastime.

Hot Spots: Both Texas and Arizona are literal "hot" spots for javelinas

Draw Status: In Texas javelina tags come with your license; in other states like Arizona they are a draw species, but generally with pretty good odds

Best Value Hunt: Almost anywhere you find them they are a good value hunt, however it seems like Texas may have nicer accommodations for the same money.

Cost: This is a hunt that can be done for well under $1,000 and that includes tags, meals, lodging and a private ranch for several days. Get a few buddies together and drive and the cost will come down even further.

BLACK BEAR

Next to whitetail deer, black bears are the most widely dispersed North American big game species. From east to west and from north to south, there are only a handful states that don't have black bears. Depending upon the state, tags are available either over the counter or as a draw, and in some places like Washington State where the bear population is exceptionally high, even non-resident hunters are allowed to buy up to two bear tags over the counter for a nominal fee. Again depending upon the state, hunters may have the opportunity to hunt spring or fall, with or without bait or dogs (baiting and running dogs has fallen under much scrutiny recently and the states that still allow it are constantly reviewing it, as to their status the best bet is to check the most recent hunting regulations.)

Hunting bears can be a lot of fun. Different methods work well in different places and at different times of the year. I have excellent hunts simply spotting openings in the forest either along an old logging road or an open hillside. I have hunted them over bait, which I found challenging and exciting (it is especially challenging

Black bears have the widest distribution of any bear species and can be hunted by several methods. Depending on where you're looking to bear hunt, they can be a draw permit, or in some states, over the counter tags are available.

if you bait them yourself) and I have called them with predator calls. However you hunt them bears provide some heart pounding excitement for do-it-yourself hunters.

JUDGING TROPHY BEARS

One of the biggest problems novice (and for that matter even experienced hunters) have when hunting black bears is judging size. Bears in general are especially tough in this regard. Without horns or antlers to compare, distinguishing a large bear from a small one can be a difficult task.

Brad Saalsaa, noted Alaskan bear guide describes a big bear like a middle aged mature man. "You want to always pay attention to the basics of bear field judging, namely the size and spacing of the ears in regards to the head, but judging a truly big bear is more than that. Look for other tell tale signs such as a swayed back, that comes from old age and a heavy frame, a sagging gut that is close to the ground and wide hips which create a swaggering walk...find all of these

Bears in Southeast Alaska grow to monsterous sizes and offer very challenging hunts. The best thing is, the tags are available over the counter. While not an easy hunt for sure, a black bear hunt is something that can be thrown together on short notice.

characteristics plus the small ears and you are probably looking at an old bear with good trophy potential. It has been my experience that trophy sized bears just act different. They are not skittish like a younger bear, but they stroll around completely secure in their surrounding – which they are if they are the dominant bear."

Bear hunting really doesn't take too much special equipment for most "normal" hunts. A standard rifle in a modest deer caliber, hunting clothes and a day pack. Often hunters can stay in area campgrounds and hike into their preferred hunting area for a day hike. This is another big game that can be done for the cost of the tag and the price of getting to the spot – not a whole lot else is required.

Hot Spots: The west has really come on with numbers of bears. Montana, Idaho Washington and Oregon are all good bear states.

Sleeper Spots: Since Washington outlawed hound and bait hunting a decade ago, the bear hunting has been phenomenal

Best Value Hunt: This also goes to Washington State – tags are ultra cheap for non-residents and they can purchase two.

Cost: This is a hunt that could be done for less than $500 from almost anywhere. Get a cheap ticket to Seattle, buy your tags, rent a car and head in any direction an hour away and you can find public property with good amounts of bears.

World Record: 23 10/16

CARIBOU

Caribou are often one of the first true adventure big game species traveling hunters target – for several reasons. The cost of the hunt is within the range of what many consider "affordable," they can be hunted without a guide and they have an extremely wide distribution from far western Alaska to the island of Newfoundland. For a trophy big game hunt it really is hard to beat a caribou. They have impressive racks, a beautiful coat that makes a beautiful hide or shoulder mount and the meat is wonderful. Add a very high hunter success rate and the opportunity to look over lots of animals before pulling the trigger and you have a recipe for a great big game hunt.

While all Canadian provinces require a guide to hunt caribou, "guiding" is a pretty loose term. Currently in some Canadian provinces a guide does not have to be right by your side, only in camp. This means you can't do a truly unguided hunt in Canada, but can come pretty close. You can drive to the destination, stay in their camp, cook your own meals, guide yourself and pack you own meat for about half of what a fully guided hunt will cost, making it a pretty affordable hunt for hunters on a budget.

In Alaska, resident and non-resident hunters alike can experience a truly wilderness experience for caribou. Several outfitters are selling unguided hunts, but they are actually an Alaska-based facilitator. They provide the camping equipment and groceries then contract with an air taxi operator (or are one themselves) to drop you into the bush. This is a great way to hunt caribou, you are left alone to set up camp, cook, and hunt, and after a week they come back in and get you. Generally speaking most of these operations have a couple of contingency policies for relocation due to lack of game, meat pick up or early retrieval that range from a mid week scheduled stop to a daily fly by. You leave different color flags on the tent to signify your status. Or you may have the use of a portable sat phone to call back to headquarters.

Another option for ultimate do it yourselfers is to contract with the air taxi yourself, provide your own food and camping equipment and save a few dollars. I do not recommend doing this – ask me how I know. I did this for my first caribou hunt. The difference between lugging my ultralight camping gear to Alaska, providing my own food and contracting with an air taxi as opposed to buying the

Caribou hunts are not all that difficult if you hit the migration right, making this a perfect hunt for a father and son to do together.

Caribou are one of the most readily available species for the do-it-yourself hunter. Alaska's Dalton highway, also known as the Haul Road, is the only place you can drive to to hunt caribou. For five miles on either side of the road is open to archery hunting only, but past that you can find caribou hunting with a rifle.

package was something like $400.00 I chose to do it myself and while it was a good experience and we shot caribou, we did not in the end save any money. To begin with there are certain items you could not bring on a commercial airliner even pre 9/11 – white gas or propane were two of these items. It was not practical to purchase food in the lower 48 and lug it all the way to Alaska. So my partner and I spent an entire day with a cabbie (meter running of course) running from the airport to the grocery store to the outdoor store, to get all of our shopping done. What we didn't realize is that loaf of bread in Alaska or a can of white gas costs significantly more than back home. Between the inflated Alaska prices, cost of the cab and the waste of time we might have saved a bit of money each – but it wasn't worth the effort. Do yourself a favor and go on this hunt, but buy it as a package with the equiptment & food thrown in..

Hot Spots: Caribou hot spots change frequently but at the time of this writing Kotzebou Alaska and Northern Quebec are producing some great bulls

Draw Status: most caribou herds are all over the counter tags.

Sleeper Spots: Manitoba has some very good bulls without as much pressure as either Alaska or Quebec.

Best Value Hunt: The best value really depends upon where you live. West coast hunters will find getting to Alaska cheaper, Midwest and eastern hunters will have a cheaper time getting to Quebec.

Cost: While published prices appear really cheap for caribou, this is a hunt that will surprise you as the travel gets expensive. Door to door with trophies in tow if you can pull it off for under $3,500 consider it a good deal. $4,000 - $5,000 is more realistic.

World Record: Mountain 453, woodland 419 5/8, barren ground 477, central Canada barren ground 433 4/8, Quebec Labrador 474 6/8

FREE RANGING NON-INDIGENOUS SPECIES/EXOTICS

Luckily for hunters looking for something different, North America has a plethora of big game available. There are even some huntable species that are not indigenous to North America – but still lots of fun to hunt. I am not talking about hunting on a high fenced game ranch, but hunting wild populations of free ranging game released or escaped into the wild years ago.

The non-indigenous species with the widest range and largest population has to be the feral pig. Found from coast to coast across the southern third of the United States, feral pigs are expanding at an alarming rate. As previously stated, feral pigs are non-indigenous to the United States, but escaped or were released from early settlers and have since bred in the wild. Since they compete with indigenous species for food and habitat they are hunted with very few to no restrictions, limits or seasons. Some of the best hunting for them can be found in Florida, Texas, Louisiana, Georgia, and Oklahoma; however good pig hunting is not limited to the southeast alone. California also has some fantastic wild pig hunting.

While pigs are the most wide spread huntable non-indigenous species in America they are not alone. The Southwest region plays home to some gorgeous antelope and goat species. Most specifically, the White Sands missile range in New Mexico has a very stable population of gemsbok (also referred to as oryx). The state conducts a draw for the permits and the odds of receiving one is not too bad. In addition to oryx, adventurous hunters can hunt for aoudad Ibex on a draw and private landowner tag basis. And you don't have to travel west or south to hunt free ranging exotics. Since 1916 Maryland has been home to a very good population of free-ranging Sitka deer. Available of two large WMA's (Taylor Island and Fishing Bay) these diminutive deer species, native to Japan can be hunted with bow, rifle or muzzleloader, making for a very unique and difficult hunt.

BISON

Bison hunting in modern America is kind of an anomaly. Of course they are a tie to our heritage, are a magnificent animal in their own right and provide hundreds of pounds of delicious, healthful meat. The downside is they are not overly challenging to hunt. Most bison hunts today are conducted on ranches with stable huntable populations of bison, and a few areas even offer true no-fence "wild" bison hunts on the boundaries of parks and wilderness areas. Hunters often debate to which is more difficult, which should be considered fair chaise and by what means they should be hunted. Like everyone I have an opinion and it is just that – an opinion and to be honest based on very little personal experience. I have been around thousands of bison in many parts of the west, have tagged along on a hunt, known hunters who have done it both ways but have not pulled the trigger myself. However I will do it someday when the mood hits me, I have some extra winter time on my hands and I have enough deep freezer space to hold the meat. What will I choose to do? To be honest, I really don't care. If I someday draw a tag and get the opportunity to hunt a "wild" herd I will do that. More than likely I will go to a large ranch

ranch in South Dakota or Wyoming, pay the rancher a fee (which is usually a lot cheaper that the fee paid to a state for a tag) and go out and shoot one. I won't kid myself it was a tough hunt, that it was a challenge or anything else. It was taking a bison for its excellent meat and getting a thick luxurious rug for the floor and a skull for my gate. Would the experience have been any different 200 years ago? I seriously doubt it. I don't think bison were overly wary to begin with. If they could be killed by the thousands by running them off a cliff or nearly driven to extinction by single shot rifles and black powder I don't think they ever presented much of a challenge. They are America's meat larder on the hoof. Appreciate the excellent food they provide, reminisce about how the West might have been and enjoy the scenery. That, in my opinion, is what bison hunting is all about.

However, if you must hunt a free ranging bison and want an animal that can be submitted to Boone and Crocket look to either the Henry Mountain or Antelope Island herd in Utah, both are classified as free ranging animals and I am told make for a slightly more challenging hunt.

Bison hunting started the drive west for most of America and still holds a nostalgic place in many hearts. Bison can still be hunted today in several states with free-ranging animals. There are also captive herds of animals that can be hunted.

CHAPTER 10

Western State Round Up

This section of the book is intended to give prospective non-resident hunters an overview of the main western hunting states and Alaska. Be aware that state's drawing procedures, license fees, and general rules and regulations can change dramatically from year to year. For this reason hunters need to use this section as a guideline, but read all material published by the individual state at the time of applying to keep informed of current changes and practices. Each state's contact information is listed in conjunction with the state for this purpose.

ARIZONA

Arizona Game and Fish Department
2221 W Greenway Rd.
Phoenix, AZ 85023
602-942-3000
www.azgfd.com

Arizona, while sometimes a difficult place to draw a tag and has very regulated opportunities for non-residents, it also has some of the best hunting for big game in the West. Almost all of them big game tags are by draw and like several other states, require that hunters purchase a hunting license before applying for a tag. By doing this, it reduces the numbers of non-resident hunters applying in the state and increases the odds of those who do. Each year, hunters that fail to draw will be awarded a bonus point. Bonus points will also be awarded for successfully taking Arizona's hunters education class as well as for 5 years of continuous applying. You can also just apply for points if you want to increase your odds in upcoming years. Arizona has been a top producer of trophy Rocky mountain big horns as well as desert sheep, elk over the 400 inch mark, tremendous mule and couse deer as well as some terrific antelope. If you are serious about getting trophy quality animals, regardless of the difficulty of drawing a tag, Arizona is a good place to apply.

Arizona at a glance

2007 non resident fees

Prices include the $7.50 application fee

Class G general hunting License $151.25
Class F Combination Hunting and Fishing license . . . $225.75
Class F youth combination Hunting and Fishing
. . . . $26.50 (before the applicants 20th birthday)
Bighorn Sheep tag. $1,407.50
Buffalo cow (bulls are not available to NR $3,262.75
Deer tag $232.75
Elk. $405.00
Sheep $1,005.00
Antelope. $330.00
Deer. $130.50

Application Process

Hunters can apply online or by mail with a paper application. Online credit cards may be used. For paper applications personal checks, cashiers check or money order will need to be sent. A hunting license must be purchased before the tag can be applied for.

Bonus points

Arizona awards bonus points for unsuccessful applicants and awards a loyalty bonus point (for hunters who have applied for 5 consecutive years starting in 2001) and a hunter education bonus point for hunters willing to travel to Arizona to take their hunter education course.

There is a non-resident cap of up to (but not guaranteed) 10% of available tags.

Group Applying

Up to four hunters may apply as a group for any species. Tags will be awarded to the entire group if there are enough in the unit.

Hunter education requirements

Youths under 14 must have a hunter education certificate. And the minimum age to hunt in Arizona is 10 years old.

Transferable Tags

There are no transferable landowner tags in Arizona at this time.

Hunter Orange

Hunter orange is not required in Arizona for big game hunting.

California

California Department of Fish and Game
3211 S Street
Sacramento, CA 95816
916-227-2245
www.dfg.ca.gov

California, while not the big game Mecca of other western states, does offer three things non-resident hunters may be interested in: Desert Big Horn Sheep, large Columbia Blacktails and feral pigs. Mule deer are also available to non resident hunters, but on a draw basis and frankly the odds and opportunities are better in other states. Like everywhere desert big horn tags are extremely limited. In California only one non-resident tag may be issued and that is not guaranteed. Obviously the odds of getting this one tag are extremely long, but if you are serious about hunting desert big horn sheep every opportunity to apply should not be overlooked.

The blacktail and pig tags are available over the counter and are a fun hunt with the blacktail season opening the earliest of all deer seasons. Keep in mind that the best hunting for both species will be found on private land and a fee will likely have to be paid.

California at a glace

2007 non-resident fees

Hunting license	$123.25
Bighorn sheep tag	$500
Elk tag fee	$1,050.00
Deer tag fee	$195.75
Antelope tag fee	$350.00
Application fee per species	$7.50

Application Process

California does not have an online application system. All applications must be mailed to their office. Applications can be paid by check, credit card, or money orders.

Preference points

Unsuccessful California applicants will receive one preference point per species. This is not dependant upon weapon, hunt, zone etc but species. Hunters not intending to hunt the current season only can also apply for preference point.

Group Applying

California does not allow hunters to apply in groups for sheep elk and antelope, however up to six hunters can apply as a party for deer.

Hunter education requirements

All hunters must show evidence of a hunter education course or show a valid hunting license issued within the last two years from any state.

Transferable tags

California does not have transferable tags available.

Minimum age to hunt

Deer, elk and antelope hunters must be 12 years only by July 1st to apply. Sheep hunters must be 16 years old by July 1st to apply.

COLORADO

Colorado Division of Wildlife
6060 Broadway
Denver, CO 80216
303-297-1192
www.wildlife.state.co.us

When it comes to hunting opportunity few western states can compete with Colorado for non-residents. A burgeoning elk herd, a remarkably rebounding mule deer population and a tag program that offers several methods of receiving tags, there is no wonder why thousands of non-residents flock to Colorado each year.

Colorado's draw system is based on preference points where hunters who don't draw a tag are awarded a preference point and the full amount of money is refunded except for a $3 fee. In addition hunters can apply for points only until such a year as they wish to draw. Not known for trophy class animals like Arizona, Colorado does offer very good chances at representative sized elk, sheep, mountain goats, moose, and antelope. The mule deer population, through sound management and mild recent winters, has rebounded well and trophy class animals are coming every year. Although not widely known, Colorado has some tremendous whitetail hunting along its far eastern border in the open plains and small river courses. Free range whitetails in the 200 inch range are a real possibility in this region.

In addition to the draw system, Colorado still offers some over the counter elk tags as well as transferable land owner tags and Ranching for Wildlife tags creating several hunting opportunities.

Colorado at a glance

2007 Non-resident fees

Application fees included in the tag price

Antelope	$304.00
Antelope youth (12-17	$103.75
Deer	$304.00
Deer, youth (12-17	$103.75
Bull Elk	$504.00
Elk, youth (12-17	$103.75
Moose	$1,719.00
Rocky Mountain Bighorn	$1,719.00
Mountain Goat	$1,719.00

Application Process

Hunters can apply online or by mail with a paper application. Online credit cards may be used. On paper applications, a personal check, cashiers check, or money order will be accepted. Each application with payment must be mailed in a separate envelope.

Preference points

Colorado has a complex preference point system. For mountain goat, moose and sheep, hunters can accumulate a maximum of three preference points (three years of applying). Until three preference points are accumulated, the odds of drawing a tag for any of these species is essentially impossible (there is not maximum number of preference points for deer, elk or antelope). After three preference points are accumulated for every unsuccessful year a bonus point is received giving the applicant an additional chance in the drawing. If you fail to apply for three years for deer, elk or antelope or five years for sheep, goat or moose you loose the preference points for that species.

Group Applying

The number of hunters applying as a group is unlimited except for sheep and goats, which have a maximum number of two hunters per application. Moose hunters are not allowed to apply as a group. The group will receive preference at the level of the group member with the fewest points. If non-residents and residents apply together, the awarded tags will be allocated from the non-resident pool (non-residents and residents may not apply together for sheep and goats).

Hunter education requirements

Anyone born on or after January 1, 1949 must complete an approved hunter education course before applying. The proof must be carried afield while hunting.

Transferable Tags

Colorado has two main types of transferable landowner licenses. The first is by draw for general landowners of over 160 acres of contiguous property. If drawn these vouchers can be given to hunters. The second type of transferable tag is the Ranching for Wildlife programs. This program was established in 1985 and guarantees participating landowners a set number of tags with liberal season dates for resident and non-resident hunters alike, in exchange for allowing resident hunters who draw tags in their unit to hunt their ranch at no charge.

Minimum age to Hunt

The minimum age to hunt big game in Colorado is 12 and there are special licenses available for youth hunters age, 12-17.

Hunter Orange

Colorado requires hunters to wear a minimum of 500 square inches of solid blaze orange above the waist line (including the head region) when hunting deer, elk, antelope, moose or bear with a muzzleloader or rifle.

IDAHO

Idaho Fish and game Department
600 S. Walnut
P.O. Box 25
Boise, ID 83707
208-334-3700

Idaho is one of only two western states that do not offer a preference point system for their draws (New Mexico is the other), but in essence they really don't need one as they have made the odds for their draws possibly the best in the west through a different means. To begin with Idaho requires all applicants to buy a hunting license just to apply (at the time of writing this was $141.50). This severely reduces the number of hunters willing/able to apply. Then they only allow applicants to apply for a sheep, goat or moose tag (only one not all three). If any of these species are applied for then a controlled hunt for deer, antelope or elk tag cannot be applied for. By doing this Idaho keeps their odds very reasonable, and in their opinion not needing a preference system. The chance of drawing a tag for goat and sheep units in Idaho have been as good as 1 in 5 in the past, and shiras moose units have been as good as 1 in a dozen. Obviously some of the prime units have much lower odds, but even then they are still better than a lot of other states.

Idaho still offers tags for deer (both mule deer and whitetails) and elk over the counter in many parts of the state and has some great hunting for both. If you are serious about hunting sheep, goats or moose Idaho is a must apply state even though it is slightly more expensive than other draw states.

Idaho at a Glance
2007 non-resident fees

Hunting license	$141.50
Bighorn Sheep	$1,765.75
Mountain goat	$1,765.75
Moose	$1,765.75
Deer	$266.25
Elk	$380.25

Application Process

Hunters can apply online or by mail with their paper application. Credit cards, personal checks, cashiers checks or money orders may be used. There is no bonus point or preference system at this time.

Group Applying

Groups of two can apply for goat, sheep and moose

Hunter education requirements

Hunter education is required if you were born on or later than January 1, 1975. Bow hunter education is required for first-time bowhunters. Hunters must prove they have held an archery only hunting license in the past.

Minimum age to Hunt

The minimum age to hunt big game is 12 in Idaho

Hunter Orange

Idaho does not have any hunter orange requirements.

MONTANA

Montana Department of Fish, Wildlife and Parks
1420 East Sixth Ave
P.O. Box 200701
Helena, MT 59620
406-444-2535
www.fwp.state.mt.us

Montana with its diverse topography and large land mass has a wide range of species including: elk, whitetail deer, mule deer, mountain goats, moose, sheep, and antelope however their tag process is unique. To begin with they offer "guaranteed" draw tags if purchased through an outfitter sponsored program. This means that you have to be hunting with that outfitter and the tags themselves cost more than standard draw tags. For general do it yourself deer/elk draw hunters, Montana may not be the best choice as applicants have to apply for and draw a general deer or elk tag before being eligible to draw a "special" limited entry hunt. This means you have to shell out a considerable amount of non-refundable money before you are allowed to even try for a quality deer or elk hunt. For this reason traveling deer and elk hunters can do better than a do it yourself hunt in Montana.

For sheep, goats and moose Montana is a must apply state if you have any interest at all in these species. At the time of this writing, Montana is currently charging $753 per species for these draw tags, plus a $20 bonus point fee. If you fail to draw you receive all the money back less the bonus point fee and $3.00 In addition to this draw, Montana is the only state that has unlimited or "over the counter" sheep units. While not widely discussed or even used there are a few reasons – first you have to decide before hand if you want to put in for a sheep draw or buy the over the counter tag. If you buy the over the counter tag, you are not eligible to draw a better unit tag or vise versa. In addition to this, the actual units are very tough to access, sheep quality is not very high and may be closed at a moments notice (even before your hunt) if the quota is reached – with no refund of the tag. While it is a unique opportunity it is most definitely not something for everyone. This is discussed further in the sheep hunting section of the book.

Montana at a Glance
2007 Non-resident fees

Conservation license $10.00
Antelope License. $205.00
Antelope multi region archery only . . . .
Special Deer A permit $5.00 (must have general deer permit)
Special deer B permit . . . .$80.00 (antlerless)
Special elk permit . . . . . $9.00 (must have general elk permit)
Archery license $10.00

Bonus point fee $20.00
General elk permit . . . .
Sheep $755.00
Goat. $755.00
Moose $755.00

Application Process

Hunters can apply online or by mail. Payments can be made with credit card, or money order, no personal checks are accepted.

Group Applying

Montana allows group applying but in limited numbers. The limit is two for elk and five for antelope. Group applying is not allowed for special deer permits.

Hunter education requirements

All hunters born after January 1, 1985 must have a hunter education certificate. Bowhunters must either have a bowhunter education course certificate or proof of holding a previous bowhunter license.

Transferable Tags

Montana has landowner tags, but they are not transferable to hunters outside the immediate family and employees.

Minimum age to Hunt

The minimum age to hunt in Montana is 12. Children who will turn 12 by the hunt date can still apply.

Hunter Orange

Hunters or those accompanying hunters must wear a minimum of 400 square inches of hunter orange above the waist.

NEVADA

Nevada Division of Wildlife
1100 Valley Rd
Reno, NV 895212
(775) 688-1500
www.huntnevada.com

Nevada, like a few other states requires that hunters purchase a hunting license before applying. In this case it is right around $140 for non-residents. However after the license is bought applying for various species is relatively straight forward and affordable. If you apply in Nevada you should apply for all. Top species include: sheep, mule deer, elk and antelope.

Nevada is considered one of the best states for desert bighorn sheep, great elk and some fantastic mule deer. While the draw odds one of ten low, much like your luck in Vegas, it is money well spent to keep applying in Nevada.

Nevada at a glance

Hunting License $142.00
Deer. $240.00
Elk $1,200.00
Antelope. $300.00
Bighorn Sheep $1,200.00
Mountain Goat $1,200.00

Application Process

Hunters can apply online or by mail. Payments can be made with credit card or money order; no out of state personal checks will be accepted. If applying online only the hunting licensee and applicable application fees will be collected unless you draw then the tag fees will be collected. If you apply through the mail all tag fees must be paid up front. Nevada has a unique system where you can apply and draw without purchasing a hunting license but no bonus points are earned. In order to buy bonus points you must buy the license, however you can also buy the license and apply for points only for $10 per species.

Group Applying

Party applying is only allowed for deer in Nevada.

Hunter education requirements

All hunter born after January 1, 1960 must have proof of a hunter education certificate. If you are a first time applicant for Nevada you must either apply on paper or go online and choose hunter education pre-registration.

Transferable Tags

Nevada does have transferable landowner tags for deer, elk and antelope and the interesting thing is you can harvest as many deer as you have tags for. So you can draw a tag and also purchase a tag for deer so you could potentially take two deer.

Minimum age to Hunt

The minimum age to hunt big game in Nevada is 12, but a parent or legal guardian must sign the application.

Hunter Orange

Nevada does not require hunter orange to be worn while big game hunting.

NEW MEXICO

New Mexico Department of Game and Fish
P.O. Box 25112
Santa Fe NM 87504
(505) 476-8000
www.wildlife.state.nm.us

New Mexico has a wide range of diversity of big game species. One can hunt Couse whitetails, elk, antelope, mule deer, free range Oryx, Ibex and Barbary sheep as well as antelope and big horn sheep. The problem with New Mexico is not the diversity it is the quantity. Unfortunately for many of their species they have very limited huntable numbers.

Like Idaho, New Mexico does not have a preference point system, this is good for hunters just starting out applying, but unrewarding for hunters who have been at it a long time. Currently New Mexico offers a portion of their non-resident tags to hunters hunting with an outfitter. An almost equal number is also offered to non-resident hunters hunting on their own. New Mexico only charges a $6 application fee per species. The good news is this makes it affordable enough for everyone to apply. The bad news is it is affordable enough for everyone to apply – making the draw odds lousy.

A small chance is better than no chance at all and you will never draw if you don't apply. For this reason, New Mexico is a good bet to apply for all species.

New Mexico at a Glance
2007 Non-resident Fees

Habitat management and Access Validation (required . $4.00
Habitat Stamp (Required for BLM or USFS access $5.00
Deer Drawing Permit. $6.00
Deer S, License $270.00
Deer, Q/HD (license. $355.00
Elk S $541.00
Elk Q, HD. $766.00
Bighorn Sheep $3,166.00
Antelope. $276.00

Oryx $1,616.00
Ibex $1,616.00
Barbary Sheep $360.00

Application Process

Hunters can apply online or by mail (attn: Special Hunts office) with their paper application. Online credit cards may be used, on paper applications personal checks, cashiers checks or money orders are accepted. There is no bonus point or preference system at this time.

Group Applying

No more than four people may apply together for deer, elk or antelope. Other draws are limited to one person per application.

Hunter education requirements

All hunters under the age of 18 must have a hunter education certificate. A bow hunter education course is not required, but is recommended by the department.

Transferable Tags

Transferable tags are available in New Mexico for elk, deer and antelope. Restrictions vary with each species.

Minimum age to Hunt

There is no minimum age to hunt in New Mexico as long as youth under 18 have passed a hunter education course.

Hunter Orange

New Mexico does not require hunter orange to be worn while big game hunting, however when hunting on military property and the youth only hunts on the Valles Caldera National Preserve hunters must wear a minimum of 244 square inches of blaze orange.

OREGON

Oregon Department of Fish and Wildlife
3406 Cherry Ave NE
Salem, OR 97303-4924
503-947-6000
www.dfw.state.or.us

Oregon like its similar counterpart, Washington, has a plethora of big game species: rocky mountain elk, Roosevelt elk, Columbia whitetails, blacktails, mule deer, Rocky Mountain big horn sheep, California big horn sheep, whitetails, antelope, bears and mule deer. While it hasn't managed its game species to the best trophy potential, it does offer some opportunities for traveling hunters.

All applicants wishing to draw a tag in Oregon must first purchase a non-refundable hunting license (at the time of this writing it is $76.50) then pay an additional $4.50 per species application fee. If a tag is drawn the amount of the tag is paid at that time. Not known for trophy mule deer and rocky mountain elk, Oregon is a good bet for hunters looking for somewhat obscure species such as blacktail deer, and Roosevelt elk and often these are available with over the counter archery tags. In addition, while the draw odds are extremely long (one in several hundred to one in a couple of thousand) it is still worth your time to apply for sheep tags since the application cost is so low with no up front tag money being required.

Oregon at a Glance

2007 non-resident fees

Hunting License	$76.50
Application fee per species	$4.50
Deer (controlled or general	$264.50
Antelope	$277.50
Elk (controlled or General	$361.50
Bighorn sheep	$1,083.50

Application Process

Hunters can apply online or by mail. Payments can be made with credit card, personal check, or money order. While first time applicants statistically can receive a tag, their bonus point system is heavily weighted to past applicants. 75% of all tags are issued to the applicant with the most points, the remaining 25% are distributed through all applicants.

Group Applying

Parties up to 18 people may apply together for elk and deer. Parties of two can apply for antelope. Bighorn sheep draws are limited to one person. Points for the party will be a rounded average of the group.

Hunter education requirements

All hunters 17 and under must have a hunter education certificate to hunt big game and it must be in their possession.

Transferable Tags

While true transferable tags are not available in Oregon, there are landowner tags available for elk and deer. Non resident hunters have to submit their application in conjunction with the landowner and hunt on that landowners property if drawn.

Minimum age to Hunt

The minimum age to hunt in Oregon is 12. Children who will turn 12 by the hunt date can still apply.

Hunter Orange

Oregon does not require hunter orange to be worn while big game hunting.

UTAH

Utah Division of Wildlife Resources
1594 West North Temple
Salt Lake City, UT 84114-6301
801 538-4700
www.wildlife.utah.gov

Utah is a fantastic state with a wide variety of trophy big game species, but like every state, it has its pros and cons for the traveling hunter. Utah is by far the cheapest state to start applying for tags, but because of this the odds of actually drawing a tag are dismally low. Like Idaho, Utah makes hunters only apply for a limited number of tags. Hunters can apply for an elk, mule deer or an antelope, but only one. Then they can apply for a desert bighorn, rocky mountain bighorn or a mountain goat, but only one. Cost for each draw is a $5.00 application charge with the tag price due if you draw. While it is always a hard choice to decide what animal you would like to put in for, with the large 350" plus class elk coming out of southern Utah in recent years I would pick elk hands down over other species. For the sheep or goat draw I personally pick desert sheep. The odds are very long, but if drawn it truly will be a once in a lifetime hunt.

Utah at a Glance

General deer	$263.00
Premium Limited Entry Deer	$563.00
Limited Entry Buck Deer	$463.00
General Elk	$388.00
Limited Entry Bull Elk	$795.00
Premium Limited Entry Elk	$1,500.00
Antelope	$288.00
Moose	$1,513.00
Bison Henry Mountains	$1,513.00
Bison Antelope Island	$2,610.00
Desert Bighorn	$1,513.00

Rocky Mountain Bighorn $1,513.00
Rocky Mountain Goat $1,513.00

Application Process

Hunters can apply online or by mail. Payments can be made with credit card, personal checks, or money order. While first time applicants statistically can receive a tag, their bonus point system is heavily weighted to past applicants. 50% of all tags are issued to the applicant with the most points, the remaining 50% are distributed through all applicants.

Group Applying

Parties up to four people may apply for limited entry deer, elk and antelope units. Bonus points for the group are averaged and rounded down. Keep in mind do not apply as a group for units that have fewer slots than your party as you will not qualify.

Hunter education requirements

All hunters born after December 31, 1965 must posses a hunter education certificate

Land Owner/Transferable Tags

There are two different types of transferable tags available to non-residents in Utah. The first is called CWMU (Cooperative Wildlife Management Unit) where landowners are issued transferable tags in conjunction for allowing access to residents, the second system is just transferable tags issued to landowners and are good for the entire unit.

Minimum age to hunt

The minimum age to hunt big game in Utah is 14. Children who will turn 14 by the hunt date can still apply.

Hunter Orange

At least 400 inches of hunter orange material must be worn on the head, chest and back while big game hunting in Utah with the exception of archery, muzzleloader and goat and sheep hunts.

WASHINGTON

Washington is worth mentioning for western hunters because of its diversity and some unique species only found in the Pacific Northwest. Washington probably has more types of big game than nearly any other state. Two species of elk, mule deer, blacktail and whitetail deer, black bears, cougars, moose, sheep and goats. With the exception of antelope Washington has it all. Most species are available as over the counter tags with the exception of moose, sheep and goats.

Washington sounds like a great place for the traveling do-it-yourself big game hunter, but there is a downside. Hunters quickly realize that Washington is far from perfect. Blessed with more diversity in habitat and species than nearly any other state, their game department does a poor job of managing the wildlife for trophy animals.

Other western states have listened to hunters and have implemented draws and other techniques to reduce pressure and increase trophy size. Washington for the most part still operates their game department like they did in the 1950's. This means overcrowded hunting areas, sub-standard trophies and weird nonresident policies. Basically the state operates with over-the-counter tags. They have tried some limited draw hunts to reduce pressure and increase trophy class however, you have to buy a hunting license and a tag before applying for a trophy unit, which is very undesirable for non-residents. If you don't draw the trophy unit you are stuck with a non-refundable hunting license/tag for a general unit. Considering they charge more for deer tags than almost any other state in the west for non-residents this doesn't exactly bode well for visiting hunters. Washington has made very it clear they don't put much emphasis on non-resident hunters or their opinions.

While poorly managed at all levels, it is still worth looking into for sheep, goats and moose. Avoid the special deer and elk draws, just hunt general season with primitive weapons to help avoid the crowds.

Washington at a Glance

Sheep	$1,095.50
Moose	$1,095.50
Goat	$1,095.50
Elk	$394.20
Deer	$394.20
Deer and Elk Combo	$613.20

Application Process

For the most part Washington is an over the counter state but for their limited species such as moose, sheep and mountain goats they are a draw which can be done on line or through the mail. For general species such as deer and elk, I don't recommend applying for trophy units unless you have a general unit you would be satisfied to hunt. If you don't draw you are forced to keep the general license/tag.

Group Applying

Party applications are accepted in Washington. A maximum of two applicants can apply for species such as sheep, goats and moose and up to five can apply for elk and deer.

Hunter education requirements

All hunters born after January 1, 1972 must have a hunter education certificate or they must prove they are not a first time hunter. A previous years license constitutes this proof.

Transferable Tags

Washington state does not have a transferable tag program.

Minimum age to hunt

There is no minimum age to hunt in Washington. Hunters must have passed an approved Hunter Education course and hunt with an adult until the age of 14.

Hunter Orange

Washington requires at least 400 square inches of hunter orange be worn above the waist while big game hunting. This is not required for archery hunting or during the sheep, goat or moose season.

WYOMING

Wyoming is an excellent state for a variety of western species. With more bighorn sheep tags issued than any other state, an abundance of moose permits, some outstanding mule deer, antelope and elk hunting opportunities this is a must apply for state. Wyoming reserves 75% of its tags for hunters with maximum points, the remaining 25% are available for the remainder of the hunters. Wyoming offers three different ways for hunters to participate in their draw. Hunters can apply for the tag, they can apply for special tags for elk, deer and antelope and they can apply for a bonus point alone. A word about the special tags. By increasing the costs of the tag in theory the draw odds should go up, but in actuality they do not always. So be sure to look at previous year's draw odds before paying the additional amount of the special license. The good news is for hunters with maximum points (currently 12) there are several units for all species that have 100% chance of drawing. When all this is considered Wyoming is a still a great state to apply for antelope, mule deer, elk and sheep. Even if you have few or no bonus points it is never too late to start.

Application Process

Wyoming is not the easiest state to apply in. They have different application deadlines for elk, deer and big horn sheep/moose. In past years these dates have been among the earliest of all application deadlines. Currently elk is due January 31, deer and antelope are due March 15, moose, bighorn sheep and goat are due February 28th. Applicants must be done through the mail. Personal checks, money orders and cashier checks are accepted.

Group Applying

Groups can apply with the maximum number being six. Groups can only apply for deer, elk and antelope.

Hunter education requirements

All hunters born after January 1, 1966 must have a hunter education certificate.

Transferable Tags

While Wyoming does issue landowner tags to residents and nonresidents alike, neither are transferable.

Minimum Hunting Age

The minimum age to hunt big game in Wyoming is 12 years old.

Hunter Orange

During the big game season hunter in Wyoming must wear one of the following blaze orange garments: hat, vest, jacket, coat or sweater

FRINGE WESTERN STATES

There are a few states that most people would not consider a true western state, but for the purpose of the traveling hunter should be included. They have some "western" species that may offer a good opportunity. North Dakota, South Dakota, and Nebraska all fall into this category. All three have huntable populations of mule deer and antelope and are available to non-resident hunters. While none of the states are known for animals of record book proportions, these states are generally easy to access, tags are available and the price is often cheaper than alternatives farther west.

In the case of Nebraska the mule deer tags are available over the counter as are the archery antelope tags. Rifle or muzzleloader antelope tags must be applied for and the odds are relatively decent of drawing either.

South Dakota has a draw for both deer and antelope, but has over the counter archery tags available for both. In addition to their standard draw, they also offer a guaranteed deer tag in select units for a higher price.

North Dakota is a real sleeper state for mule deer. Available only by draw in the western portion of the state, some nice sized mule deer come from the Bad Lands region. Typically comprised of public land or relatively easy to access private land, North Dakota offers mule deer hunters some terrific opportunities.

ALASKA

Our farthest "western" state and our last true frontier, Alaska deserves a book written entirely dedicated to its big game species and hunting opportunities, but in light of this book intent; namely the affordable do it yourself big game species, Alaska can be summarized rather shortly. While containing a wide variety of big game species the only ones that can be hunted by a non-resident without a guide are caribou, moose, black bears, wolf, wolverine and blacktail deer. But these species in and of themselves are enough to last a lifetime. While there are some draw units specifically for moose, most of Alaska's big game tags are available over the counter. The reality of Alaska however is that even doing it yourself is not cheap. Alaska is simply an expensive place to hunt if you want to have quality hunting. Most good hunting regions are either very remote or simply hard to get to and if there is an easy way to access them, you will quickly find out that you are not alone. There will be other hunters. Due to the very limited road network the main modes of transportation in Alaska are by either light plane or boat and hiring either can become expensive. Remote camps are the order of the day, but for hunters looking for a little more comfort at bargain prices the USFS cabins that are available for a nominal fee are a great option. Alaska is a great state to hunt as a non-resident and a do it yourselfer, but you must be prepared for the task. This means be in good shape and experienced enough to be completely self reliant. Packing up camp and driving back into town for a hot meal and a warm room are seldom an option in our last frontier.

For first timers to Alaska looking to do it alone, at the time of this writing I would suggest a spring black bear hunt, a caribou hunt in the interior or a blacktail deer hunt on Kodiak island. Any of these hunts can be done completely by yourself, with a transporter or with a guide and all are an economical way to hunt Alaska for the first time.

References and Resources

The most important thing to have when planning your dream hunting adventure is knowledge. The rules and regulations are vital, as is knowing where to get the correct gear to match what you have in mind.

Federal Offices

The federal government is a good place to go when looking for information. Whether you're looking for a list of accessible lands, topographic maps, park access, or basic regulations and advice, the government is a logical place to start. Below are the top offices that have helped me throughout the years.

The U.S. Fish and Wildlife Service
www.fws.gov

U.S. Bureau of Land Management, Office of Public Affairs
1849 C Street, Room 406-LS
Washington, DC 20240
Phone: (202) 452-5125
Fax: (202) 452-5124
www.blm.gov

The National Park Service
www.nps.gov

U.S. Department of the Interior
1849 C Street, NW
Washington, DC 20240
www.doi.gov

United State Geological Survey
www.usgs.gov

HUNTER EDUCATION REQUIREMENTS

The International Hunter Education Association provided information for this section on hunter education requirements. They can be found on the web at www. ihea.com.

State Information

Each state has its own agency dealing fish, wildlife and other natural resources. Remember as a responsible hunter, you must know the rules and regulations of each state you pan to hunt. It is also a good idea to make sure you follow all the rules for transporting game form one state to another.

Alabama

Anyone born on or after August 1, 1977 must show proof of completing a Hunter Education course prior to purchasing a hunting license except active duty U.S. military personnel, Alabama residents who are active members of the National Guard of the United States, and persons certified by the Alabama Peace Officers Standards and Training Commission as law enforcement officers who are employed by a law enforcement agency.

State Agency Contact Information
Division of Wildlife and Freshwater Fisheries
Dept. of Conservation and Natural Resources
64 N. Union Street, Suite 584
P.O. Box 301457, Montgomery, AL 36130-1457
(334) 242-3469
www.outdooralabama.com

Alaska

Hunter Education Certification is required for young hunters in Units 7, 13, 14, 15, and 20. If you are under 16 years of age, you must have either successfully completed a Basic Hunter Education course or be under the direct immediate supervision of a licensed hunter who is (a) 16 years of age or older and has successfully completed a certified hunter education course, OR (b) born on or before January 1, 1986. If you are 16 years of age or older AND were born after January 1, 1986 you must have successfully completed a Certified Hunter Education Course before you can hunt. In addition, all hunters must complete a Hunter Education Certification class before hunting in these areas: Eagle River Management Area for black bear & small game, Anchorage Coastal Wildlife Refuge, Mendenhall Wetlands State Game Refuge if under age 15 or be accompanied by an adult, Palmer/Wasilla Management area (shotgun for big game), and all army military lands. Hunters in weapons restricted areas (archery, muzzleloading, or shotgun) must complete a state-approved certification course for that weapon. Weapons certification does not satisfy general Hunter Education Certification requirements and visa versa.

State Agency Contact Information
  Alaska Department of Fish & Game
  P.O. Box 115526
  1255 W. 8th Street
  Juneau, AK 99811-5526
  www.adfg.state.ak.us

Arizona

Hunter Education graduation is required for 10 to 14 year-olds who wish to hunt big game.

State Agency Contact Information
  Arizona Game and Fish Dept., Game Branch
  221 W. Greenway Road, Phoenix, AZ 85023
  (602) 942-3000
  www.gf.state.az.us

Arkansas

To hunt, you must have successfully completed an approved Hunter Education course if you were born after December 31, 1968.

State Agency Contact Information
  Arkansas Game and Fish Commission
  #2 Natural Resources Drive, Little Rock, AR 72205
  (800) 364-4263
  www.agfc.com

California

All hunting license buyers must have either a CA license, a hunting license from another state that is not more than 2 hunting years old, or H/E certification from CA or another state or province.

State Agency Contact Information
  Department of Fish and Game Headquarters
  1416 9th Street, Sacramento, CA 95814
  (916) 445-0411
  www.dfg.ca.gov

Colorado

Required of anyone born on or after January 1, 1949 to purchase any hunting or trapping license.

State Agency Contact Information
Colorado Division of Wildlife
6060 Broadway, Denver, Colorado, 80216
(303) 297-1192
http://wildlife.state.co.us/

Connecticut

Firearms Hunting: Certificate required of all persons regardless of age who have not held a resident firearms license in the past five years or for a first time licensee. Bowhunting: Connecticut Advanced Bowhunter Education Certificate or its equivalent (NBEF/IBEP content) from another state required for all archery permit applicants. Previous resident bowhunting license does not qualify.

State Agency Contact Information
Connecticut Dept. of Environmental Protection
79 Elm Street, Hartford, CT 06106-5127
(860) 424-3000
www.ct.gov/dep/site/default.asp

Delaware

All persons born after Jan. 1, 1967, must satisfactorily complete a Hunter Education course before obtaining a Delaware Hunting License.

State Agency Contact Information
State of Delaware Division of Fish and Wildlife
4876 Hay Point Landing Road. Smyrna, DE 19977
(302) 739-9910
www.dnrec.state.de.us

Florida

Hunter Education is required of all persons born on or after June 1, 1975.

State Agency Contact Information
Fish and Wildlife Conservation Commission
Farris Bryant Building, 620 S. Meridian St.
Tallahassee, FL 32399-1600
(850) 488-4676
http://myfwc.com/

Hawaii

To purchase a Hunting License you must have completed an approved Hunter Education course. A "Letter of Exemption" can be issued if you were born "before" January 1, 1972, and can provide proof of a "Hawaii" hunting license purchased before July 1, 1990.

State Agency Contact Information
Department of Land and Natural Resources
Kalanimoku Building
1151 Punchbowl St.
Honolulu, HI 96813
www.state.hi.us/dlnr
(808) 587-0167

Georgia

Residents and non-residents born on or after Jan.1, 1961, must successfully complete a hunter education course before purchasing a season hunting license. However, a hunter education course is not required to purchase a one (1) day or seven (7) day hunting license. Hunters age 12-15 must complete a hunter education course before hunting unless under supervision of a licensed adult hunter. Hunters age 12-15 must be under adult supervision while hunting on a WMA. Hunters under age 12 are not required to complete a hunter education course, unless hunting on National Wildlife Refuges (NWRs), or Park Services lands, children 10-16 must carry a valid hunter safety certificate. Hunter education is not required to hunt on one's own land or land of a parent or guardian.

State Agency Contact Information
   Georgia Dept. of Natural Resources, Commissioner's Office
   2 Martin Luther King, Jr. Dr., S. E.,
   Suite 1252 East Tower, Atlanta, GA 30334
   (404) 656-3500
   http://georgiawildlife.dnr.state.ga.us/

Idaho

To purchase a hunting license you must have completed an approved Hunter Education course if you were born after January 1, 1975.

State Agency Contact Information
   Fish and Game Department
   Box 25, Boise, ID 83707
   (208) 334-3700
   http://fishandgame.idaho.gov

Illinois

To purchase a hunting license you must have completed an approved Hunter Education course if you were born on or after January 1, 1980.

State Agency Contact Information
   Department of Natural Resources
   One Natural Resources Way, Springfield, IL 62702
   (217) 782-6302
   www.dnr.state.il.us/

Indiana

If you were born after December 31, 1986, you must complete a certified hunter education course.

State Agency Contact Information
   Indiana Division of Fish and Wildlife
   402 W. Washington Street, Room W273
   Indianapolis, IN 46204
   (317) 232-4080
   www.in.gov/dnr/fishwild/hunt/

Iowa

To purchase a hunting license you must have completed an approved Hunter Education course if you were born after January 1, 1967.

State Agency Contact Information
Department of Natural Resources
502 E. 9th Street, Des Moines, IA 50319
(515) 281-5918
www.iowadnr.com

Kansas

Anyone born on or after July 1, 1957 must successfully complete a certified hunter education course in order to hunt in Kansas.

State Agency Contact Information
Kansas Dept. of Wildlife & Parks Operations Office
512 SE 25th Ave., Pratt, KS 67124
(620) 672-5911
www.kdwp.state.ks.us

Kentucky

All hunters born after Jan. 1, 1975, shall have a valid hunter education card IN POSSESSION WHILE HUNTING. A card is not needed for purchase. Exceptions: 1) Children under 10 may hunt without a card if accompanied by an adult. 2) Persons exempt from a hunting license are also exempt from hunter education card requirements (i.e., landowners; military on furlough).

State Agency Contact Information
Kentucky Dept. of Fish and Wildlife Resources
#1 Sportsman's Lane, Frankfort, KY 40601
(800) 858-1549
www.kyafield.com

Louisiana

Any person born on or after Sept. 01, 1969 must have proof of completion of a hunter education course to purchase a hunting license.

State Agency Contact Information
Department of Wildlife & Fisheries
2000 Quail Drive, Baton Rouge, LA 70808
(225) 765-2800
www.wlf.state.la.us

Maine

Applicant for an adult hunting license must show proof of having previously held an adult license to hunt with firearms in any year beginning with 1976 or successful completion of an approved hunter safety course from this or any other state. To obtain an adult archery-hunting license, you must show proof of having held an adult license to hunt with bow and arrow in any year after 1979 or successful completion of an archery education course. To obtain a crossbow permit, you must complete crossbow education or have proof of having hunted in another state that allowed crossbow use.

State Agency Contact Information
Dept. of Inland Fisheries and Wildlife
284 State Street, 41 State House Station
Augusta, ME 04333-0041
(207) 287-8000
www.maine.gov/ifw

Maryland

To purchase a hunting license you must have completed an approved Hunter Education course unless you hunted prior to July 1, 1977; three-day non-resident waterfowl hunters are exempted.

State Agency Contact Information
Maryland Department of Natural Resources
580 Taylor Avenue, Tawes State Office Building
Annapolis, MD 21401
(877) 620-8367
www.dnr.state.md.us

Massachusetts

It shall be unlawful for any resident or non-resident to hunt for any bird or mammal in the commonwealth unless such person has successfully completed a hunter education course as prescribed by this section, or unless such person held a license to hunt before January 1, 2007.

State Agency Contact Information
Department of Fish and Game
251 Causeway St. #400, Boston, MA. 02114
(617) 626-1500
http://mass.gov/dfwele/

Michigan

You must take hunter safety if you were born after January 1, 1960. A hunter safety certificate or previous hunting license is required to purchase any Michigan Hunting License. Hunters anticipating an out-of-state hunting trip need to obtain a certificate prior to their trip, most states require hunters to carry their certificate when hunting and need it to purchase a license.

State Agency Contact Information
Wildlife Office, Department of Natural Resources
Mason Building, P.O. Box 30444, Lansing MI 48909
(517) 373-1263
www.michigan.gov/dnr

Minnesota

Hunter Education is required of all persons born after December 31, 1979 in order to purchase a big or small game-hunting license.

State Agency Contact Information
DNR State Agency Contact Information Center
500 Lafayette Road, St. Paul, MN 55155-4040
(651) 296-6157 or (888) 646-6367
www.dnr.state.mn.us/hunting/deer/

Mississippi

Hunter Education is mandatory for all persons born on or after January 1, 1972, and plans to purchase a Mississippi hunting license. Also, anyone 12-16 years old must have a certificate of satisfactory completion of a hunter education course approved by the department before hunting in this state. Anyone under the age of 12 must be in the presence and under the direct supervision of a licensed or exempt hunter at least 21 years of age when the child is hunting.

State Agency Contact Information
Department of Wildlife, Fisheries and Parks
1505 Eastover Drive, Jackson, MS 39211-6374
(601) 432-2400
www.mdwfp.com

Missouri

Any person born on or after January 1, 1967 shall obtain and display an approved Hunter Education certificate card prior to purchase of any firearms hunting permit. Minimum age is 11 to take and be certified by the course, youth under 16 must provide birth certificate as proof of age.

State Agency Contact Information
Missouri Department of Conservation
P.O. Box 180, Jefferson City, MO 64192-0180
(573) 751-4115
www.mdc.mo.gov

Montana

Effective Oct. 1, 2003, anyone born after Jan. 1, 1985 must have a hunter education card to purchase a Montana hunting license. We honor cards from all states and provinces.

State Agency Contact Information
Montana Fish, Wildlife and Parks
1420 E 6th Ave., Box 200701, Helena, MT 59620
(406) 444-2535
http://fwp.mt.gov/

Nebraska

Certificate of completion of a hunter and/or bowhunter education course is required to be carried on your person while hunting, by everyone age 12 or older born on or after January 1, 1977. Under age 12 must be in the company of a licensed adult 19 or older for all hunting with firearm or cross bow, age 12 thru 15 can only hunt deer, antelope, elk or mountain sheep while in the company of an adult 21 or older.

State Agency Contact Information
Nebraska Game and Parks Commission
2200 N. 33rd Street, Box 30370, Lincoln, NE 68503
(402) 471-0641
www.ngpc.state.ne.us

Nevada

Anyone born after Jan. 1, 1960, must show proof of Hunter Education each time they purchase a hunting license. Proof of Hunter Education is: An official original or duplicate Hunter Education certificate, or a past year's hunting license with a Hunter Education number or unique mark signifying Hunter Education.

State Agency Contact Information
Nevada Department of Wildlife Headquarters
1100 Valley Rd.
Reno, NV 89512
(775) 688-1500
http://ndow.org

New Hampshire

To purchase a hunting license you must have completed an approved Hunter Education course, or provide proof that you have previously held a hunting license in any state or province. Hunters and trappers in New Hampshire must attend training courses specific to the license type they wish to purchase. By state law, anyone planning to buy a basic hunting license, archery license or trapping license must complete the respective hunter, bowhunter or trapper education course. Individuals may purchase each of these licenses by showing a certificate of completion from the appropriate course, or a previously issued license of the same type.

State Agency Contact Information
  New Hampshire Fish and Game Department
  11 Hazen Drive, Concord, NH 03301
  (603) 271-3511
  www.wildlife.state.nh.us

New Jersey

Hunter Education is mandatory for all first-time firearms hunters. Students 10 to 15 years of age are issued a free youth license, which includes a pheasant stamp, upon completion of the course. While hunting, youths ages 10 to 13 must be accompanied by a properly licensed adult 21 years of age or older. If you lose your hunting or trapping license and had never taken a hunter education course, you must also take one of these courses.

State Agency Contact Information
  N.J. Division of Fish and Wildlife
  P.O. Box 400, Trenton, NJ 08625-0400
  (609) 292-2965
  www.state.nj.us/dep/fgw

New Mexico

Hunter Education is required of persons under the age of 18 before hunting with or shooting a firearm.

State Agency Contact Information
  New Mexico Department of Game and Fish
  P.O. Box 25112
  Santa Fe, NM 87504
  (505) 476-8000
  www.wildlife.state.nm.us

New York

All hunters, regardless of age, are required to present either a hunter education certificate or a previous hunting license to qualify for a license.

State Agency Contact Information
  Dept. of Environmental Conservation Bureau of Wildlife
  625 Broadway, Albany, NY 12233
  (518) 402-8924
  www.dec.ny.gov

North Carolina

No person, regardless of age, may procure a hunting license or hunt in this state with out first producing a certificate of competency showing completion of a hunter safety course or a hunting license issued prior to July 1, 1991, or a signed statement (shown on the license) that he or she had such a license.

State Agency Contact Information
  Wildlife Resources Commission Division of Wildlife Management
  1722 Mail Service Center, Raleigh, NC 27699
  (919) 707-0010
  www.ncwildlife.org

North Dakota

All persons born after 1961 shall submit or exhibit a certificate of successful completion of a hunter education course before purchasing any hunting license. A certificate of completion for the same course of study issued by other states, provinces or countries is valid in North Dakota.

State Agency Contact Information
  North Dakota Game and Fish Department
  100 N. Bismarck Expressway,
  Bismarck, ND 58501-5095
  (701) 328-6300
  http://gf.nd.gov/

Ohio

To purchase a hunting license you must have completed an approved Hunter Education course or present evidence of having previously held a hunting license.

State Agency Contact Information
Ohio Dept. of Natural Resources, Division of Wildlife
2045 Morse Rd., Bldg. G,
Columbus, OH 43229-6693
(800) 945-3543
www.ohiodnr.com/wildlife

Oklahoma

To purchase a hunting license you must have completed an approved Hunter Education course if you were born on or after January 1, 1972.

State Agency Contact Information
Department of Wildlife Conservation
Box 53465, Oklahoma City, OK 73152-3465
(405) 521-3851
www.wildlifedepartment.com

Oregon

All persons under 18 years of age must possess a hunter education certificate while hunting any species by any means, except when hunting on own property or parent's property.

State Agency Contact Information
Department of Fish and Wildlife
3406 Cherry Avenue N.E., Salem, OR 97303
(503) 947-6000
www.dfw.state.or.us

Pennsylvania

To purchase a hunting license you must complete an approved Hunter Education course, if you have not held a hunting license in this Commonwealth or another state or nation.

State Agency Contact Information
Pennsylvania Game Commission
2001 Elmerton Avenue, Harrisburg, PA 17110-9797
(717) 787-4250
www.pgc.state.pa.us

Rhode Island

To purchase a hunting license you must have completed an approved Hunter Education course unless you present evidence of holding a prior years Rhode Island license.

State Agency Contact Information
Department of Environmental Management
277 Great Neck Rd., West Kingston, RI 02892
(401) 789-0281
www.dem.ri.gov

South Carolina

All residents and nonresidents born after June 30, 1979, must successfully complete a hunter education course that is approved by the Department of Natural Resources before a hunting license can be obtained.

State Agency Contact Information
Department of Natural Resources
P. O. Box 167, Columbia, SC 29202
(803) 734-3888
www.dnr.sc.gov

South Dakota

To purchase a hunting license you must have completed an approved Hunter Education Course if you are under the age of 16.

State Agency Contact Information
South Dakota Game, Fish and Parks
412 West Missouri, Pierre, SD 57501
(605) 773-3485
www.sdgfp.info

Tennessee

If born on or after Jan 1, 1969, must have proof of successfully completing a hunter education course.

State Agency Contact Information
Tennessee Wildlife Resources Agency
Box 40747, Nashville, TN 37204
(615) 781-6500
www.state.tn.us/twra

Texas

Every hunter (including out-of-state hunters) born on or after Sept. 2, 1971, must successfully complete a Hunter Education Training Course. Minimum age of certification is 12 years and cost is $15. If you were born on or after Sept. 2, 1971, and you are under 12 years of age, you must be accompanied. If you are age 12 through 16, you must successfully complete a hunter education course or be accompanied. If you're age 17 and over, you must successfully complete a hunter education course; or purchase a Hunter Education Deferral, and be accompanied. Hunter Education Deferral (cost: $10) allows a person 17 years of age or older who has not completed a hunter education program to defer completion for up to one year. A deferral may only be obtained once and is only valid until the end of the current license year. A person who has been convicted or has received deferred adjudication for violation of the mandatory hunter education requirement is prohibited from applying for a deferral. Take the course by August 31 of the current license year and receive a $5 discount. Accompanied means: By a person (resident or non-resident) who is at least 17, who is licensed to hunt in Texas, who has passed hunter education or is exempt (born before Sept. 2, 1971), and you must be within normal voice control, (Preferably within physical control). Proof of certification or deferral is required to be on your person while hunting. Note: Certification is NOT required to purchase a hunting license. Note: Bowhunter education does NOT substitute for Hunter Education certification.

State Agency Contact Information

Texas Parks and Wildlife Department
4200 Smith School Road, Austin, TX 78744
(800) 792-1112
www.tpwd.state.tx.us

Utah

A person born after December 21, 1965, may not purchase a hunting license or permit unless proof is presented to the Division or one of its authorized wildlife license agents that the person has passed a Division-approved hunter education course offered by a state, province or country.

State Agency Contact Information
Utah Division of Wildlife Resources
Box 146301
Salt Lake City, UT 84114-6301
(801) 538-4700
http://wildlife.utah.gov

Vermont

An applicant for a hunting license must present either a previous or current hunting license from any state or Canadian province, or a certificate or letter of proof showing satisfactory completion of an approved hunter or firearms safety course from Vermont or any other state or province, or other satisfactory proof of prior license or hunter/firearms safety certification.

State Agency Contact Information
Vermont Fish and Wildlife Department
10 South, 103 South Main St., Waterbury, VT 05671
(802) 241-3700
www.vtfishandwildlife.com

Virginia

To purchase a hunting license you must have completed an approved Hunter Education course if you are twelve to fifteen years of age, or sixteen and over and have never held a license to hunt.

State Agency Contact Information
Department of Game and Inland Fisheries
P O Box 11104, Richmond, VA 23230-1104
(804) 367-1000
www.dgif.state.va.us

Washington

All first-time hunters purchasing their first Washington license and who are born after 1/1/72 must complete an approved hunter education course.

State Agency Contact Information
Washington Department of Fish and Wildlife
600 Capitol Way N., Olympia, WA 98501-1091
(360) 902-2200
http://wdfw.wa.gov/

West Virginia

A hunting license may not be issued to any person who was born on or after Jan. 1, 1975, unless the person submits to the license agent a certificate of training or proof of completion of a course approved by the I.H.E.A. or Director of WV DNR 20-2-30a.

State Agency Contact Information
Wildlife Resources
State Capitol, Building 3, Charleston, WV 25305
(304) 558-2771
www.wvdnr.gov

Wisconsin

To purchase a hunting license you must have completed an approved Hunter Education course if you were born on or after January 1, 1973.

State Agency Contact Information
Wisconsin Department of Natural Resources
Bureau of Wildlife Management (WM/6)
101 S. Webster Street, Box 7921
Madison, WI 53707-7921
(608) 266-2621
www.dnr.state.wi.us

Wyoming

NO person born on or after Jan. 1, 1966, may apply for and receive any Wyoming hunting license, NOR take any wildlife by the use of firearms on land other than that of his own family, unless the person possesses and can exhibit a certificate of competency and safety in the use and handling of firearms.

State Agency Contact Information
Wyoming Game and Fish Department
5400 Bishop Blvd., Cheyenne, WY 82006
(307) 777-4600
http://gf.state.wy.us/

Canada
Alberta

Hunter Education is mandatory for 12 & 13 year olds. Anyone 14 and older can challenge the First Time Hunter Test or take the Hunter Education course.

Province Contact information
Information Centre
Main Floor, 9920 108 Street
Edmonton, Alberta
Canada T5K 2M4
Phone: 310 0000 (toll free anywhere in Alberta)
     (780) 427 2711 (outside of Alberta)
     www.srd.alberta.ca

British Columbia

Youth ages 10-13 may hunt with a junior hunting license, no education requirement. At 14 years of age, the Conservation and Outdoor Education (CORE) program, BC hunter education program is mandatory. All youth less than 19 years of age must be accompanied by a licensed adult hunter. A licensed guide must accompany non-residents hunting big game. No education course required to get a non-resident hunting license.

Province Contact information
Ministry of the Environment, Fish and Wildlife Branch
Phone: 250-387-9711
Fax: 250-387-9568
Mail: PO Box 9391, STN PROV GOVT
     Victoria, B.C. V8W 9M8
E-mail: www.envmail@gov.bc.ca

Manitoba

Students must be a minimum of twelve years of age. All first-time hunters (including bowhunters) must show proof of having taken the Manitoba Hunter and Firearm Safety Course OR a similar course from another province or state. Hunter Education became mandatory in Manitoba in 1969, therefore anyone purchasing a hunting license who was not 19 years of age in 1969 and had not previously held a hunting license, must have the Hunter Education training requirements.

Province Contact information
Manitoba Conservation
Tel: 204-945-3744
Fax: 204-945-4261
Toll Free in North America: 1-866-MANITOBA
(1-866-626-4862)
TTY: 204-945-4796
E-mail: mgi@gov.mb.ca

Newfoundland and Labrador

All New Hunters must complete the Firearm Safety/Hunter Education Program prior to applying for a Big or Small game license.

Province Contact information
Department of Environment and Conservation
4th Floor, West Block
Confederation Building
P.O. Box 8700
St. John's NL Canada A1B 4J6

Telephone: 709-729-2664
Fax: 709-729-6639
Toll Free: 1-800-563-6181
E-mail: info@gov.nl.ca

Nova Scotia

To purchase a hunting license you must have completed an approved Hunter Education course.

Province Contact information

Street address:
NS Dept. of Natural Resources
1701 Hollis Street
Founders Square
Halifax, NS B3J 3M8

Mailing address:
P.O. Box 698
Halifax, NS B3J 2T9
Canada

General Inquiries
Fax: 902-424-5935
902-424 7735

Northwest Territory

A license to hunt big game will not be issued to anyone under the age of 16 years. A license to hunt small game may be issued to a person between 14 and 16 years of age. If a person intends to hunt small game in the NWT and is 14 or 15 years old, in addition to possessing a small game-hunting license:

a) They must be accompanied by a parent or guardian who holds a hunting license for small game, and
b) The parent or guardian must endorse the application and license for small game.

Parents or guardians who endorse the application are responsible for the activities of a minor while hunting.

Province Contact information

Northwest Territories Tourism
(http://www.explorenwt.com/)
Box 610
Yellowknife, NT, Canada X1A 2N5
Toll free: 1-800-661-0788
Outside North America: (867) 873-7200
Fax: (867) 873-4059
E-mail: dyan@spectacularnwt.com
www.nwtwildlife.com/hunting/

New Brunswick

All hunters born on or after January 1, 1981 and all first time hunters must complete a Firearm Safety/Hunter Education course. Bow hunters are also required to complete a Bow Hunter Education course. Students must be 13 years of age to participate in the Firearm Safety/Hunter Education program. Conservation Education certificates from other states or provinces are recognized by New Brunswick.

Province Contact information

Hugh John Flemming Forestry Centre
P. O. Box 6000
Fredericton, NB
E3B 5H1
Canada
General Information: (506) 453-2207
Reception: (506) 453-2207
Fax: (506) 444-5839
Web Site: http://www.gnb.ca/0078/index-e.asp

Ontario

Hunter Education Stand Alone course is minimum of 12.5 hours of instructor-based education. A "One Stop" course combines the Canadian Firearms Safety Course and Hunter Education Course. Minimum 20 hours of instruction. * Ontario residents may hunt at 15 years of age provided they have parental consent. The Hunter Apprenticeship Safety Program (HASP) allows residents (12 yrs and older) to participate under the direct and immediate supervision of a qualified mentor following the successful completion of a hunter education course and examination. Participants must share one firearm and have parental consent if under the age of 16.

Province Contact information
   Ontario Ministry of Natural Resources Information Centre,
   300 Water St., P.O. Box 7000,
   Peterborough, Ont. K9J 8M5
   General Inquiries (English):
   1-800-667-1940
   General Inquiries (French):
   1-800-667-1840
   E-mail: mnr.nric@mnr.gov.on.ca
   Web Site: www.mnr.gov.on.ca
   Outdoors Card Renewal Line: 1-800-288-1155
   Maps, aerial photos, or government
   Publications: 1-800-667-1940.

Quebec

To purchase a hunting license to hunt with a firearm, a bow or a crossbow, residents must have successfully completed an approved Hunter Education course. To trap, residents must have successfully completed an approved Trapper Education course. The requirements to obtain a hunter's or a trapper's certificates are: be a Quebec resident, be at least 12 years of age and not have had the said certificate suspended or cancelled following a Court conviction. A person must accompany anyone under the age of 16 for bow or crossbow hunting, and 18 for firearm hunting, 18 years of age or older who is the holder of a hunter's certificate appropriate with the arm used or a non-resident's hunting license. Under the "Federal Firearm Act," for firearm hunting, anyone who doesn't have a firearm possession license must be under the presence and immediate supervision of a person who is in lawful possession of the firearm.

Province Contact information
  Service aux citoyens et aux entreprises
  880, chemin Sainte-Foy, RC 120-C
  Québec (Québec) G1S 4X4
  Téléphone : 418 627-8600
  Ligne sans frais : 1 866 248-6936, 1 866 CITOYEN
  Télécopieur : 418 644-6513
  Courriel : service.citoyens@mrnf.gouv.qc.ca

Prince Edward Island

All hunters hunting on Prince Edward Island are required to be in possession of a Firearm Safety Certificate from any province or state. 1) All first time hunters and all individuals born on or after September 1, 1968 are required to successfully complete a Firearm/ Hunter Safety Course. 2) All individuals who were born before September 1, 1968, and who have hunted previously can apply for a P.E.I. Firearm Safety Certificate by signing an affidavit.

Province Contact information
  Island Information Service
  P.O. Box 2000
  Charlottetown, PE
  Canada C1A 7N8
  (902) 368-4000
  island@gov.pe.ca

For toll-free tourism information, phone
1-800-463-4PEI.
Saskatchewan
The province requires mandatory hunter education for anyone wishing to hunt regardless of age.

Province Contact information
  1-800-567-4224 (toll free in Saskatchewan)
  953-3750 in Prince Albert
  inquiry@serm.gov.sk.ca

Regina Office
3211 Albert Street
Regina, Saskatchewan
S4S 5W6

Forest Service
1061 Central Avenue
Prince Albert, Saskatchewan
S6V 6G1

Yukon

As a non-resident of the Yukon, in the summer you can hunt rabbits, ground squirrels and porcupines on your own without a licensed guide. In the fall, (after September 1) you can also hunt grouse, ptarmigan and waterfowl without a guide.

Small game

Small game hunting licenses are available at Environment Yukon offices and selected sporting goods stores. You'll receive a copy of the Yukon Hunting Regulations Summary when you pick up a license.

Migratory birds

You must have a valid permit to hunt migratory birds such as ducks and geese. Migratory bird hunting permits are available at federal postal outlets throughout the Yukon. You will receive a copy of the migratory bird hunting regulations when you obtain your permit. Open season for most migratory birds runs from September 1 to October 31.

Big game

You can hunt big game animals in the Yukon only if you are outfitted by a licensed outfitter and accompanied by a licensed big game guide. Big game animals include moose, caribou, mountain sheep, mountain goat, black bear, grizzly bear, wolf, coyote and wolverine. For a list of big game outfitters contact the Yukon Outfitters Association.

Sign up for the free Hunter Education and Ethics Development (HEED) workshop. The 20-hour workshop is held throughout the year in most Yukon communities, depending on enrollment. Topics include firearm safety, wilderness survival, wildlife identification, hunting regulations, wildlife management and outdoor ethics.

Separate workshops are also offered for moose, sheep, bear and bison hunters. These workshops provide hunting tips as well as information about identification, meat care, ethics and regulations.

Young first-time hunters born after April 1, 1987 must successfully complete this course before being issued a hunting license.

Province Contact information

Government of Yukon
Box 2703
Whitehorse, Yukon
Y1A 2C6
Telephone: 867-667-5811 or 867-667-5812
information@gov.yk.ca

Hunter Orange Requirements

A ll information provided by the International Hunters
Education Association www.ihea.com

United States

Alabama

All hunters during gun deer season must wear a vest or cap with at least 144 square inches of solid Hunter Orange, visible from all sides. Deer hunters in tree stands elevated more than 12 feet from the ground need not wear Hunter Orange, except when traveling to and from tree stands. Only Hunter Orange, Blaze Orange or Ten Mile cloth is legal. (Exception: waterfowl, turkey and dove hunters and those hunting legally designated species during legal right time hours.)

Alaska

Upland and big game hunters are strongly recommended to wear Hunter Orange.

Arizona

Upland and big game hunters are strongly encouraged to wear Hunter Orange.

Arkansas

It shall be unlawful to hunt any wildlife, or to accompany or assist anyone in hunting wildlife, during a gun or muzzle-loading deer season without wearing an outer garment above the waistline, of daylight fluorescent blaze orange (Hunter Orange) within the color range of 595nm - color range of 555nm - 565nm (Hunter Safety Green) totaling at least 400 square inches, and a fluorescent blaze orange or fluorescent chartreuse head garment must be visibly worn on the head. EXCEPTIONS: (1) While migratory bird hunting. (2) While hunting in areas in which hunting of deer with guns is prohibited. PENALTY: $50.00 to $1,000.00.

California

Upland and big game hunters are strongly recommended to wear Hunter Orange.

Colorado

It is unlawful to not wear at least 500 square inches of solid (camouflage orange is not legal; mesh garments are legal, but not recommended) daylight FLUORESCENT ORANGE material in an outer garment above the waist, part of which must be a hat or head covering visible from all directions while hunting deer, elk or antelope during any muzzleloading rifle or rifle seasons. BOW HUNTERS ARE NOT REQUIRED TO WEAR ORANGE DURING THE ARCHERY ONLY SEASONS.

Connecticut

No person shall hunt any wildlife from September 1 through the last day of February without wearing at least a total of 400 square inches of fluorescent orange clothing above the waist visible from all sides. This color requirement shall not apply to archery deer hunting when: 1. During the separate archery deer seasons. 2. On private lands during the private land muzzleloader season and 3. On private lands in Deer Management Zones 11 and 12 during the firearms deer seasons when hunting from an elevated tree stand at least 10 feet from the ground (orange is required when walking to and from the stand); to archery and firearms turkey hunting; to waterfowl hunters hunting from blinds or a stationary position; to hunting raccoon and opossum from one-half hour after sunset to one-half hour before sunrise; or to deer hunting by a landowner on his own property.

Delaware

During a time when it is lawful to take deer with a firearm, any person hunting deer in this State shall display on his head, chest and back a total of not less than 400 square inches of Hunter Orange material.

Florida

All deer hunters, and those accompanying them, on public lands during open deer season must wear at least 500 square inches of Hunter Orange on an outer garment above the waist. (Exception: bow hunters during bow season.)

Hawaii

"Hawaii Administrative Rules Title 13-Chapter 122-12 (f)(2)" with regard blaze-orange garments while hunting of game birds: With the exception of Spring Turkey Hunting or designated archery areas, no person shall hunt, serve as a guide, accompany, or assist a hunter in any hunting area, where firearms are permitted, without wearing an exterior garment (shirt, vest, jacket, or coat) made of commercially manufactured, blaze-orange material or solid blaze-orange mesh material with a maximum mesh size of one-eighth inch. (All types of camouflage orange are prohibited for these garments.) When carrying game or wearing a backpack, the blaze-orange on the upper torso must be visible from both front and back. Hawaii Administrative Rules Title 13-Chapter 123-22 (g)(1) addresses blaze-orange garments while hunting game mammals: No person shall hunt, serve as a guide, accompany, or assist a hunter in any hunting area where firearms are permitted without wearing an exterior garment (shirt, vest, jacket, or coat) made of commercially manufactured, solid blaze-orange material or solid blaze-orange mesh material with a maximum mesh size of one-eighth inch. (All types of camouflage orange are prohibited for these garments.) When carrying game or wearing a backpack, the blaze orange on the upper torso must be visible from both front and back.

Georgia

All dear, bear and feral hog hunters, and those accompanying them, during firearm deer seasons must wear at least 500 square inches of Hunter Orange on outer garments above the waist.

Idaho

Not required. The wearing of hunter orange is strongly recommended for upland and big game hunters.

Illinois

It is unlawful to hunt or trap any species, except migratory waterfowl, during the gun deer season in counties open to gun deer hunting when not wearing 400 square inches of solid blaze orange plus a hat. It is unlawful to hunt upland game (pheasant, rabbit, quail or partridge) when not wearing a hat of solid blaze orange.

Indiana

Deer (bow and gun), rabbit, squirrel, grouse, pheasant, and quail hunter must wear at least one of the following solid Hunter Orange garments: vest, coat, jacket, coveralls, hat or cap. (Exception: bow hunters for deer until firearms season starts.)

Iowa

A person shall not hunt deer with firearms unless the person is at the time wearing one or more of the following articles of visible, external apparel: A vest, coat, jacket, sweatshirt, sweater, shirt, or coveralls, the color and material of which shall be solid blaze orange. A person shall not hunt upland game birds, as defined by the department, unless the person is at the time wearing one or more of the following articles of visible, external apparel: A hat, cap, the color and material of which shall be at least fifty percent solid blaze orange. Upland birds include pheasants, quail, partridge, ruffed grouse, and woodcock.

Kansas

Big game clothing requirements: (a) Each individual hunting deer or elk and each individual assisting an individual hunting deer or elk, shall wear Hunter Orange clothing having a predominant light wave length of 595-605 nanometers; (b) The bright orange color shall be worn as follows: 1) a hat with the exterior of not less than 50 percent of the bright orange color, an equal portion of which is visible from all directions; 2) a minimum of 100 square inches of the bright orange color on the front of the torso; and 3) a minimum of 100 square inches of the bright orange color on the back of the torso.

Kentucky

Hunter orange garments shall be worn by all deer hunters while hunting on any location on property where any deer gun season is permitted by regulations. Garments shall be worn as outer coverings on at least the head, chest and back. They shall be of a solid, unbroken pattern. Any mesh weave opening shall not exceed 1/4 inch by measurement. Garments may display a small section of another color. Camouflage pattern hunter orange garments do not meet these requirements.

Louisiana

Any person hunting deer shall display on his head, chest, and/or back a total of not less than four hundred square inches of material of a daylight fluorescent orange color known as "hunter orange" during the open gun deer hunting season. Persons hunting on privately owned, legally posted land may wear a cap or a hat that is completely covered with hunter orange material in lieu of the foregoing requirements to display four hundred square inches of hunter orange. These provisions shall not apply to persons hunting deer from elevated stands on property which is privately owned and legally posted, or to archery deer hunters, hunting on legally posted land where firearm hunting is not permitted by agreement of the owner or lessee.

Maine

Anyone who hunts with a firearm during any open firearm season on deer is required to wear two articles of solid-colored hunter orange clothing (fluorescent orange) which is in good and serviceable condition and which is visible from all sides. One article must be a hat. The other must cover a major portion of the torso, such as a jacket, vest, coat, or poncho. Regulations for 1991 still require that anyone who hunts in the moose hunting district during the moose season must wear one article of solid Hunter Orange clothing.

Maryland

All hunters and those accompanying them must wear either: 1) a cap of solid daylight fluorescent orange color; 2) a vest or jacket containing back and front panels of at least 250 square inches of solid daylight fluorescent orange color. Maryland requires 50% of Camouflage Hunter Orange garment to be daylight fluorescent orange color; or 3) an outer garment of camouflage fluorescent orange worn above the waist which contains at least 50% daylight fluorescent orange color. (Exception: Hunters of wetland game birds, fur bearing mammals, doves, crows, wild turkeys, bow hunters during archery season only, falconers, and unlicensed hunters o their own property.

Massachusetts

All hunters during shotgun deer season and deer hunters during primitive firearm season must wear at least 500 square inches of Hunter Orange on their chest, back, and head. (Exception: waterfowl hunters in a blind or boat.) All hunters on Wildlife Management Areas during pheasant and quail season must wear a Hunter Orange hat or cap. (Exception: waterfowl hunters in a blind or boat, and raccoon hunters at night.)

Michigan

All firearm hunters on any land during daylight hunting hours must wear a hat, cap, vest, jacket, rainwear, or other outer garment of Hunter Orange visible from all sides. All hunters, including archers, must comply during gun season. Camouflage Hunter Orange is legal provided 50% of the surface area is solid Hunter Orange. (Exception: waterfowl, crow, dove, and wild Turkey hunters, and bow hunters for deer during open archery season. Michigan requires 50% of a Camouflage Hunter Orange garment be open Hunter Orange.

Minnesota

A person may not hunt or trap during the open season where deer may be taken by firearms under applicable laws and ordinances, unless the visible portion of the person's cap and outer clothing above the waist, excluding sleeves and gloves, is blaze orange. Blaze orange includes a camouflage pattern of at least 50 percent blaze orange within each foot square. This section does not apply to migratory waterfowl hunters on waters of this state or in a stationary shooting location or to trappers on waters of this state. In addition to requirements already mentioned a person may not take small game other than turkey, migratory birds, raccoons, and predators, except when hunting with nontoxic shot or while trapping, unless a visible portion of at least one article of the person's clothing above the waist is blaze orange. Minnesota requires 50% of a Camouflage Hunter Orange garment be open Hunter Orange.

Mississippi

All deer hunters during any gun season for deer must wear in full view at least 500 square inches of solid, unbroken Hunter Orange visible from all sides.

Missouri

During firearm deer season, all hunters must wear a cap or hat, and a shirt, vest or coat having the outermost color be Hunter Orange and must be plainly visible from all sides while being worn. Camouflage orange garments do not meet this requirement. (Exception: Department of Conservation areas where deer hunting is restricted to archery methods.

Montana

All big game hunters and those accompanying them must wear at least 400 square inches of Hunter Orange above the waist. A hat or cap alone is not sufficient. (Exception: bow hunters during special archery season.)

Nebraska

All deer, antelope, mountain sheep or elk hunters using firearms including muzzleloaders must wear at least 400 square inches of Hunter Orange on the head, back, and chest. Upland game hunters are strongly recommended to wear Hunter Orange. Separate Bow hunter education certificate required for everyone hunting deer, antelope, elk or mountain sheep with bow and arrow born on or after January 1,1977.

Nevada

Upland and big game hunters are strongly recommended to wear Hunter Orange.

New Hampshire

Upland and big game hunters are strongly recommended to wear Hunter Orange.

New Jersey

All hunters with firearms for deer, rabbit, hare, squirrel, fox or game birds must wear a cap of solid Hunter Orange or other outer garment with at least 200 square inches of Hunter Orange visible from all sides. (Exception: waterfowl, wild turkey and bow hunters.)

New Mexico

Upland and big game hunters are strongly recommended to wear Hunter Orange.

New York

Upland and big game hunters are strongly recommended to wear Hunter Orange.

North Carolina

Any person hunting game animals other than foxes, bobcats, raccoons, and opossums, or hunting upland game birds other than wild turkeys, with the use of firearms, must wear a cap or hat on his head made of Hunter Orange materials or an outer garment of Hunter Orange, visible from all sides. (Exception: landowners hunting on their own land.)

North Dakota

Every person, while hunting big game, shall wear a head covering and an outer garment above the waistline, both of daylight fluorescent orange color, totaling 400 square inches or more and both to be worn conspicuously on the person. This section does not apply to any person hunting big game with bow and arrow during special bow hunting seasons. Additionally, while the muzzleloader and the deer gun seasons are in progress in an area, all big game hunters, including bow hunters, are required to wear a head covering and an outer garment above the waistline of solid daylight fluorescent orange color, totaling at least 400 square inches.

Ohio

Hunting any wild animal (except waterfowl) in the daylight during deer gun season, the statewide primitive deer season, and the special area primitive deer season is unlawful unless the hunter is visibly wearing a vest, coat, jacket, or overalls that are either solid hunter orange or camouflage hunter orange.

Oklahoma

All firearm deer, elk or antelope hunters must wear a head covering and outer garment above the waist with at least 500 square inches of clothing of which 400 square inches must be Hunter Orange. The camouflage orange pattern is legal as long as there is at least 400 square inches of daylight fluorescent orange. All other hunters must wear either a head covering or outer garment of Hunter Orange during open gun deer season. (Exception: waterfowl, crow, or crane hunters, and those hunting furbearing animals at night.)

Oregon
Upland and big game hunters are strongly recommended to wear Hunter Orange.

Pennsylvania
All fall small game, turkey, bear and deer hunters during the regular firearm deer season, and special archery deer season hunters during any portion of the archery season that coincides with the general small game or turkey seasons, must wear at least 250 square inches of hunter orange material on the head, chest and back combined. Spring turkey hunters must wear a minimum of 100 square inches of hunter orange on the head or back and chest while moving from one location to another. Groundhog hunters must wear 100 square inches of hunter orange on the head. All required hunter orange must be visible in a 360-degree arc. (Exceptions waterfowl, mourning dove, crow, flintlock deer season and archery season hunters except as specified.)

Rhode Island
Solid daylight fluorescent orange is required statewide, and must be worn above the waist and be visible in all directions. Examples that meet the orange requirements are a hat that covers 200 sq. in. or a combination of hat and vest covering 500 sq. in. The following orange requirements apply: 200 sq. in. by small game hunters during the small game season; 200 sq. in. by muzzleloader hunters during the muzzleloader season; 200 sq. in. by archers when traveling to/from stands during muzzleloading season; 500 sq. in. by all hunters (including archers) and all Management Area users during shotgun deer season. Exemptions: Waterfowl hunters while hunting from a boat or blind, over water or field, when done in conjunction with decoys; Crow hunters, when hunting over decoys; Turkey hunters; First segment dove hunters. In addition to above requirements, all other users (hikers, bicyclists, horseback riders, etc.) of State Management Areas are required to wear 200 sq. in. of solid daylight fluorescent orange from the third Saturday in October to the last day of February annually, and during the established mourning dove season and wild turkey season.

South Carolina

On all WMA lands and lands within the Central Piedmont, Western Piedmont and Mountain Hunt Units during the gun hunting season for deer, all hunters must wear either a hat, coat, or vest or solid visible international orange. Hunters are exempt from this requirement while hunting for dove, duck and turkey. Small game hunters while hunting at night or on privately owned lands within the hunt unit are also exempt.

South Dakota

All big game hunters with firearms must wear one or more exterior Hunter Orange garments above the waist. (Exception: turkey hunters.)

Tennessee

All big game hunters with firearms must wear at least 500 square inches of Hunter Orange on a head covering and an outer garment above the waist, visible front and back. (Exception: turkey hunters during gun hunts proclaimed by the commission and those hunting on their own property.)

Texas

All hunters and persons accompanying a hunter on National Forests and Grasslands must wear a minimum of 144 square inches of Hunter Orange visible on both the chest and back plus a Hunter Orange cap or hat. Call the US Forest Service and US Army Corps of Engineers for more information.

Utah

A person shall wear a minimum of 400 square inches of hunter orange material while hunting any species of big game. Hunter orange material must be worn on the head, chest, and back. A camouflage pattern in hunter orange does not meet the requirements of Subsection (1)(a). A person is not required to wear hunter orange material during an archery, muzzle-loader, or bighorn sheep hunt, unless a centerfire rifle hunt is in progress in the same area.

Vermont
Upland and big game hunters are strongly recommended to wear Hunter Orange.

Virginia
Hunters during firearm deer season and those accompanying them must wear Hunter Orange on the upper body, visible from all sides, or a Hunter Orange hat, or display 100 square inches of Hunter Orange within body reach, at shoulder level or higher, visible from all sides.

Washington
All hunters must wear fluorescent Hunter Orange clothing with a minimum of 400 square inches of fluorescent Hunter Orange exterior, worn above the waist and visible from all sides. (Exception: Persons who are hunting upland game bird during an upland game bird season with a muzzle-loading firearm, bow and arrow or falconry.)

West Virginia
All deer hunters during deer gun season must wear at least 400 square inches of Hunter Orange on an outer garment.

Wisconsin
All hunters during any firearms deer season must have 50% of their outer garments above the waist, including any head covering, colored Hunter Orange. (Exception: waterfowl hunters.) Wisconsin accepts camouflage orange, though solid Hunter Orange is recommended.

Wyoming
All big game hunters must wear one or more exterior garments (i.e. hat, shirt, jacket, coat, vest, or sweater) of Hunter Orange. (Exception: bow hunters during special archery season.)

Canada

Alberta

No garment color requirements or recommendations.

British Columbia

No garment color requirements or recommendations.

Manitoba

Big game hunters must wear a solid blaze orange hat and an additional 2580 sq. cm. of blaze orange above the waist and visible from all sides. Bow hunters are exempt during bow hunting seasons or in bow hunting areas only. Wolf hunters are exempt when hunting in game hunting areas while no other big game season is on. Black bear and wolf hunters are exempt during the spring season. Manitoba requires 50% of Camouflage Hunter Orange garment to be daylight fluorescent orange color.

Newfoundland and Labrador

Upland and big game hunters are strongly recommended to wear a minimum of 2580 square centimeters of Hunter Orange (400 square inches).

Nova Scotia

All hunters and those accompanying them must wear a cap or hat and a vest, coat, or shirt of solid Hunter Orange visible from all sides. Camouflage Hunter Orange is permitted during bow hunter season for deer as long as there are at least 400 square inches visible from all sides. Nova Scotia refuses to recognize Camouflage Hunter Orange as a legal fabric except during archery deer season.

Northwest Territory

Upland and big game hunters are strongly recommended to wear Hunter Orange.

New Brunswick

Every person, while hunting or being a licensed guide accompanying any person engaged in hunting shall wear a hat and upon his or her back, chest and shoulders, an exterior garment of which not less than 2580 square centimeters (400 square inches) in aggregate shall be exposed to view in such a manner as to be plainly visible from all directions, and the color of the hat and the exterior garment shall be solid hunter orange.

Ontario
All hunters must wear a minimum of 2580 square centimeters (400 square inches) of solid Hunter Orange clothing above the waist that is visible from all sides and head cover during the Deer, Moose and Bear gun-hunting seasons. Exceptions include bear hunters, while hunting from an elevated stand, bow hunters during bows only seasons and waterfowl hunters.

Quebec
All hunters, guides and companions must wear at least 2580 square centimeters (400 square inches) of Hunter Orange on their back, shoulders, and chest, visible from any angle. During hunting season through December 1st, coyote, fox and wolf hunters and guides are required to wear the same as other hunters. (Exception: crow, or migratory bird hunters, and those hunting deer or moose during special archery seasons.)

Prince Edward Island
All upland game hunters are encouraged to wear Hunter Orange.

Saskatchewan
All big game hunters must wear a complete outer suit of scarlet, bright yellow, Hunter Orange or white, and a head covering of any of these colors except white. (Exception: bow hunters and black powder hunters during special archery muzzle-loading seasons.)

Yukon
No garment color requirements or recommendations.

REPLACING LOST HUNTER EDUCATION CARDS

I've done it and many folks I know have done it. You take a hunter's safety course when you're young and then don't think about it again. But then you up and move and you find you need that card again. Perhaps you're planning a hunt and realize you need it for the state you're headed to, or just find that it has been misplaced and want to have it just in case. The following list of contacts can help you get things back on track.

Provided by www.IHEA.com

United States

- **Alabama**
Agency Site: http://www.outdooralabama.com
Hunter Education Site: http://www.outdooralabama.com/hunting/education/
Replacement Certification Card: http://www.outdooralabama.com/hunting/education/cards.cfm

- **Alaska**
Agency Site: http://www.state.ak.us/local/akpages/FISH.GAME/
Hunter Education Site: http://www.wildlife.alaska.gov/education/huntered/huntered.cfm
Replacement Certification Card: No web access, must call office

- **Arizona**
Agency Site: http://www.azgfd.gov
Hunter Education Site: http://www.azgfd.gov/h_f/hunting.shtml
Replacement Certification Card: No web access, must call office at 602-789-3235

- **Arkansas**
Agency Site: http://www.agfc.com/
Hunter Education Site: http://www.agfc.com/huntereducation/index.html
Replacement Certification Card: www.agfc.com/education/hunter_education_details.html#Card

- **California**
Agency Site: http://www.dfg.ca.gov/
Hunter Education Site: http://www.dfg.ca.gov/huntered/index.html
Replacement Certification Card: http://www.dfg.ca.gov/huntered/index.html#Replace

- **Colorado**
Agency Site: http://www.wildlife.state.co.us/
Hunter Education Site: http://www.wildlife.state.co.us/Hunting/Hunter Education
Replacement Certification Card: http://wildlife.state.co.us/Hunting/HunterEducation/CardReplacement/

- **Connecticut**
  Agency Site: http://www.ct.gov/dep/cwp/view.asp?a=27
  00&q=323414&depNav_GID=1633
  Hunter Education Site: http://www.ct.gov/dep/cwp/
  view.asp?a=2222&q=320790&depNav_GID=1633
  Replacement Certification Card: No web access, must call
  office
- **Delaware**
  Agency Site: http://www.fw.delaware.gov
  Hunter Education Site: http://www.fw.delaware.gov/
  HunterEd/HunterEd.htm
  Replacement Certification Card: No web access, must
  contact office
- **Florida**
  Agency Site: myfwc.com
  Hunter Education Site: myfwc.com/huntersafety
  Replacement Certification Card: At MyFWC.com/Hunter
  Safety follow the "print duplicate card" link on the right-
  hand side of the screen.
- **Georgia**
  Agency Site: http://www.gadnr.org/
  Hunter Education Site: http://www.gohuntgeorgia.com/
  content/displaynavigation.asp?TopCategory=7
  Replacement Certification Card: http://georgiawildlife.dnr.
  state.ga.us/content/displaynavigation.asp?TopCategory=7
- **Hawaii**
  Agency Site: http://www.state.hi.us/dlnr/
  Hunter Education Site: http://www.state.hi.us/dlnr/dcre/
  home.htm
  Replacement Certification Card: http://www.state.hi.us/
  dlnr/dcre/home.htm
- **Idaho**
  Agency Site: http://fishandgame.idaho.gov/
  Hunter Education Site: http://fishandgame.idaho.gov/
  cms/education/hunter_ed/
  Replacement Certification Card: Located on IDFG web site
  (http://fishandgame.idaho.gov/education/hunter_ed/
  replace_card.cfm) or contact office

- **Illinois**
  Agency Site: http://dnr.state.il.us/
  Hunter Education Site: http://dnr.state.il.us/safety
  Replacement Certification Card: http://dnr.state.il.us/
  lands/education/safety/index.htm
- **Indiana**
  Agency Site: http://www.in.gov/dnr
  Hunter Education Site: http://www.in.gov/dnr/lawenfor/
  hunt-edu.htm
  Replacement Certification Card: http://www.in.gov/dnr/
  lawenfor/education/hunt-edu.htm or contact office
- **Iowa**
  Agency Site: http://www.iowadnr.com/
  Hunter Education Site: http://www.iowadnr.com/law/
  hunter/index.html
  Replacement Certification Card:
- **Kansas**
  Agency Site: http://www.kdwp.state.ks.us/
  Hunter Education Site: http://www.kdwp.state.ks.us/
  news/hunting/hunter_education
  Replacement Certification Card: https://www.
  accesskansas.org/app/kdwp/hunt_ed/index.php
- **Kentucky**
  Agency Site: http://www.kdfwr.state.ky.us/
  Hunter Education Site: http://www.kdfwr.state.ky.us/
  navigation.asp?cid=145&NavPath=C117
  Replacement Certification Card: http://www.kdfwr.state.
  ky.us/navigation.asp?cid=291&NavPath=C117C145
- **Louisiana**
  Agency Site: http://www.wlf.state.la.us/
  Hunter Education Site: http://www.wlf.state.la.us/
  hunting/education/
  Replacement Certification Card: http://www.wlf.state.
  la.us/hbscards/hbscards1.asp
- **Maine**
  Agency Site: http://www.state.me.us/ifw/
  Hunter Education Site: http://www.state.me.us/ifw/
  education/safety/index.htm
  Replacement Certification Card: No web access, may call
  office but will need written request: mail request, fax to 207-
  287-5220 or email brenda.chaplin@maine.gov with request

- **Maryland**
  Agency Site: http://www.dnr.state.md.us/
  Hunter Education Site: http://www.dnr.state.md.us/nrp/education/index.html
  Replacement Certification Card: http://www.dnr.state.md.us/nrp/education/index.html
- **Massachusetts**
  Agency Site: http://www.state.ma.us/dfwele/dfw
  Hunter Education Site: http://www.state.ma.us/dfwele/dfw/dfwhecl.htm
  Replacement Certification Card: http://www.mass.gov/dfwele/dfw/dfwhuntr.htm#DUPS
- **Michigan**
  Agency Site: http://www.michigan.gov/dnr
  Hunter Education Site: http://www.michigandnr.com/hunting/recnsrch.asp
  Replacement Certification Card: http://www.michigandnr.com/hunting/recnsrch.asp
- **Minnesota**
  Agency Site: http://www.dnr.state.mn.us/
  Hunter Education Site: http://www.dnr.state.mn.us/safety/firearms/index.html
  Replacement Certification Card: No web access, must contact office
- **Mississippi**
  Agency Site: http://www.mdwfp.com/
  Hunter Education Site: http://www.mdwfp.com/level2/Education/Huntered.asp
  Replacement Certification Card: http://www.mdwfp.com/hunting_edu.asp
- **Missouri**
  Agency Site: http://www.mdc.mo.gov/
  Hunter Education Site: http://www.mdc.mo.gov/hunt/huntered/
  Replacement Certification Card: No web access, must contact office
- **Montana**
  Agency Site: http://fwp.mt.gov
  Hunter Education Site: http://fwp.state.mt.us/education/huntereducation/default.html
  Replacement Certification Card: http://fwp.state.mt.us/education/huntereducation/hunterprog.html#cert2

- **Nebraska**
  Agency Site: http://www.ngpc.state.ne.us/
  Hunter Education Site: http://www.ngpc.state.ne.us/
  hunting/programs/education/firearm.asp
  Replacement Certification Card: http://www.ngpc.
  state.ne.us/huntin/programs/education/dupinfo.
  asp?ClassType=bow
- **Nevada**
  Agency Site: http://www.ndow.org
  Hunter Education Site: http://ndow.org/learn/classes/
  hunt/
  Replacement Certification Card: No web access, must
  contact office
- **New Hampshire**
  Agency Site: http://www.wildlife.state.nh.us/
  Hunter Education Site: http://www.wildlife.state.nh.us/
  Hunting/hunter_ed.htm
  Replacement Certification Card: No web access, must
  contact office
- **New Jersey**
  Agency Site: http://www.state.nj.us/dep/fgw/
  Hunter Education Site: http://www.state.nj.us/dep/fgw/
  hunted.htm
  Replacement Certification Card: http://www.state.nj.us/
  dep/fgw/hntedupe.htm
- **New Mexico**
  Agency Site: http://www.wildlife.state.nm.us
  Hunter Education Site: http://www.wildlife.state.nm.us/
  education/hunter_ed/index.htm
  Replacement Certification Card: Duplicate cards available
  on the Departments web site, www.wildlife.state.nm.us
  under the education tab.
- **New York**
  Agency Site: http://www.dec.state.ny.us/
  Hunter Education Site: http://www.dec.state.ny.us/
  website/dfwmr/sportsed/index.html
  Replacement Certification Card: Call 1-888-HUNT-ED2

- **North Carolina**
  Agency Site: http://www.ncwildlife.org
  Hunter Education Site: http://www.ncwildlife.org/fs_
  index_08_education.htm
  Replacement Certification Card: E-mail nancy.boykin@
  ncwildlife.org
- **North Dakota**
  Agency Site: http://www.gf.nd.gov
  Hunter Education Site: same
  Replacement Certification Card: Duplicate card can be
  ordered on website.
- **Ohio**
  Agency Site: http://www.ohiodnr.com/wildlife
  Hunter Education Site: http://www.ohiodnr.com/wildlife/
  Hunting/huntered/instructor.htm
  Replacement Certification Card: No web access, must
  contact office
- **Oklahoma**
  Agency Site: http://www.wildlifedepartment.com/
  Hunter Education Site: http://www.wildlifedepartment.
  com/FAQs.htm#faqhe
  Replacement Certification Card: http://www.
  wildlifedepartment.com/CARD.HTM
- **Oregon**
  Agency Site: http://www.dfw.state.or.us/
  Hunter Education Site: http://www.dfw.state.or.us/
  outdoor_skills/
  Replacement Certification Card: No web access, must
  contact office
- **Pennsylvania**
  Agency Site: http://www.pgc.state.pa.us/
  Hunter Education Site: http://www.pgc.state.pa.us/pgc/
  cwp/view.asp?a=461&q=153086
  Replacement Certification Card: http://www.pgc.state.
  pa.us/pgc/cwp/view.asp?a=460&q=158266#htecard
- **Puerto Rico**
  Agency Site: www.drna.gobierno.pr
  Hunter Education Site:
  Replacement Certification Card:

- **Rhode Island**
  Agency Site: http://www.state.ri.us/dem/programs/bnatres/fishwild/
  Hunter Education Site: http://www.state.ri.us/dem/programs/bnatres/fishwild/huntered/index.htm
  Replacement Certification Card: Contact the Hunter Education Office at (401) 789-3094.
- **South Carolina**
  Agency Site: http://www.dnr.sc.gov/
  Hunter Education Site: http://www.dnr.sc.gov/education/hunted.html
  Replacement Certification Card: Contact agency directly
- **South Dakota**
  Agency Site: http://www.sdgfp.info/
  Hunter Education Site: http://www.sdgfp.info/Wildlife/hunting/Safety/HuntSAFEIndex.htm
  Replacement Certification Card: Can find information at: http://www.sdgfp.info/Wildlife/hunting/Safety/NewHuntersafetycard.htm
- **Tennessee**
  Agency Site: http://www.tnwildlife.org
  Hunter Education Site: http://www.state.tn.us/twra/hntclass.html
  Replacement Certification Card: No web access, must contact office
- **Texas**
  Agency Site: http://www.tpwd.state.tx.us/
  Hunter Education Site: http://www.tpwd.state.tx.us/learning/hunter_education/
  Replacement Certification Card: http://www.tpwd.state.tx.us/learning/hunter_education/cardform.phtml
- **Utah**
  Agency Site: http://www.wildlife.utah.gov
  Hunter Education Site: http://www.wildlife.utah.gov/huntereducation/
  Replacement Certification Card: No web access, must contact office

- **Vermont**
  Agency Site: http://www.vtfishandwildlife.com
  Hunter Education Site: http://www.vtfishandwildlife.com/HE_Courses.cfm
  Replacement Certification Card: No web access, must call office
- **Virginia**
  Agency Site: http://www.dgif.state.va.us/
  Hunter Education Site: http://www3.dgif.virginia.gov/ClassSchedule/Outline.aspx?dept=Hunting&text=t
  Replacement Certification Card: Call 1-877-HUNT-EDU
- **Washington**
  Agency Site: http://wdfw.wa.gov/
  Hunter Education Site: http://wdfw.wa.gov/enf/huntered/
  Replacement Certification Card: http://wdfw.wa.gov/enf/huntered/certificate.htm
- **West Virginia**
  Agency Site: http://www.wvdnr.gov/
  Hunter Education Site: http://www.wvdnr.gov/lenforce/education.shtm
  Replacement Certification Card: http://www.wvdnr.gov/lenforce/education.shtm
- **Wisconsin**
  Agency Site: http://www.dnr.state.wi.us/
  Hunter Education Site: http://www.dnr.state.wi.us/org/es/enforcement/safety/hunted.htm
  Replacement Certification Card: No web access, must contact office
- **Wyoming**
  Agency Site: http://gf.state.wy.us/
  Hunter Education Site: http://gf.state.wy.us/services/education/huntered/index.asp
  Replacement Certification Card: No web access, must contact office

Canada

- **Alberta**
  Agency Site: http://www.aheia.com
  Hunter Education Site: http://www.aheia.com
  Replacement Certification Card: Must call 403-252-8474, only have files on graduates from 1997 on
- **British Columbia**
  Agency Site: http://www.bcwf.bc.ca/
  Hunter Education Site: http://www.bcwf.bc.ca/programs/core/index.html
  Replacement Certification Card: Contact office
- **Manitoba**
  Agency Site: http://www.mwf.mb.ca
  Hunter Education Site: http://www.mwf.mb.ca/hunter_ed.htm
  Replacement Certification Card: No web access, contact office
- **New Brunswick**
  Agency Site: http://www.gnb.ca/0078/f&w/
  Hunter Education Site: http://www.gnb.ca/0078/f&w/huntered/index.htm
  Replacement Certification Card: http://www.gnb.ca/0078/fw/huntered/repcard.asp
- **Newfoundland and Labrador**
  Agency Site: http://www.gov.nl.ca/env/wildlife/default.htm
  Hunter Education Site: http://www.gov.nf.ca/env/wildlife/edu-train/index.htm
  Replacement Certification Card: No web access, must contact office
- **Northwest Territory**
  Agency Site: http://www.nwtwildlife.rwed.gov.nt.ca/
  Hunter Education Site:
  Replacement Certification Card:

- **Nova Scotia**
  Agency Site: http://www.gov.ns.ca/NATR/
  Hunter Education Site: http://www.gov.ns.ca/NATR/hunt/hunting.htm
  Replacement Certification Card: No web access, must contact office
- **Ontario**
  Agency Site: http://www.ohep.net
  Hunter Education Site: http://www.ohep.net
  Replacement Certification Card: 1-800-667-1940
- **Prince Edward Island**
  Agency Site: http://www.gov.pe.ca/infopei/index.php3?number=16940&lang=E
  Hunter Education Site: http://www.gov.pe.ca/infopei/index.php3?number=16940&lang=E
  Replacement Certification Card:
- **Quebec**
  Agency Site: http://www.fapaq.gouv.qc.ca/en/index1.htm
  Hunter Education Site: http://www.fapaq.gouv.qc.ca/en/educ/formatio.htm
  Replacement Certification Card:
- **Saskatchewan**
  Agency Site: http://www.sasktelwebsite.net/safee/
  Hunter Education Site: http://www.sasktelwebsite.net/safee/
  Replacement Certification Card: No web access, must contact office
- **Yukon**
  Agency Site: http://www.environmentyukon.gov.yk.ca/main/index.shtml
  Hunter Education Site: http://www.environmentyukon.gov.yk.ca/hunting/heed.html
  Replacement Certification Card: No web access, must contact office

Specialty Big Game Hunting Gear

Hunting big game can be physically demanding and having the right gear can make the difference between a successful, comfortable hunt and tough one. The products I have listed below are just a small sampling of what is available, but made my list as they are proven, well made and ideal for any dream hunt.

The Leupold RXB-IV Laser rangefinding binoculars offer the hunter the convienience of a high-quality pair of binoculars with their amazing True Balistic Range laser rangefinding technology. For wide-open terrain, these bino's are the way to go.

The Green Ring Boone and Crocket Club binoculars from Leupold are top notch for anyone looking for a classic hunting binocular.

Leupold
www.leupold.com

Leupold makes all types of excellent optics from binoculars, to spotting scopes to riflescopes to rangefinders. They offer a wide variety of prices, styles and models to suit any big game hunter.

Kifaru

www.kifaru.net

Kifaru is an extremely interesting company obsessed with removing excess weight in anything they produce. From packs, to tents to stoves and even rifles Kifaru makes some of the best hunting products on the market and almost always the lightest weight.

Eberlestock

www.eberlestock.com

This company has its roots in Olympic level biathlon rifle stocks and equipment, but also makes some of the most incredible packs for hauling out large bulky loads such as elk quarters. Their packs are designed to be collapsed down when not hauling large loads and easily expanded when game is on the ground – idea for those that want just one pack that can do anything.

When you've got to carry a heavy load, or pack out both an animal and your rifle, the Gunslinger from Eberlestock is hard to beat.

Mystery Ranch

www.mysterranch.com

Another excellent pack company with a similar philosophy – get into and out of the backcountry with just one pack. As ideal for carrying camping equipment in as it is for carrying meat out, these are well-designed packs for backcountry hunters.

When you're going deep into the backcountry, you need lots of gear. That's where Mystery Ranch packs come in. Perfect for when you've got to haul it all.

Wiggy's

www.wiggys.com

Wiggy's sleeping bags have long been used by serious outdoorsmen, guides and hunters due to their unique insulating material, Lamilite. Their bags can be modified to perform exceptionally well under a wide range of temperature extremes.

ACR

www.acrelectronics.com

ACR is a maker of personal locator products from the relatively simple reflection mirror and flashing emergency strobe to the highly sophisticated locator satellite beacon. A must have for extremely remote hunters.

The latest personal locator beacons can direct help to your location anywhere in the world.

Katadyn

www.katadyn.com

With many styles and types of water purifiers available Katadyn makes a unit that will work perfect for you, making virtually all water drinkable.

All it takes is one microscopic bug to turn a fun trip into a terrible one. Katadyn's backcountry filters are the easiest way to make water safe.

The Vario filter pump has different filter stages for different conditions. It is compatible with most water bottles and is perfect for 1-2 people.

Remington Arms

www.remington.com

With several styles of Model Seven and 700s available Remington makes rifles that are ideally suited for the big game hunter, and if they don't produce exactly what you desire, their custom shop very likely does.

The Model 770 is an awesome choice for the hunter on a budget. It is the perfect choice for any hunter looking to fast-forward through the process of selecting a scope and components. It comes with a pre-mounted and boresighted 3-9x40mm riflescope. But most importantly, it's built to Reminton's standards for accuracy and reliability. Simply choose your ammo and you're ready to shoot.

The Remington Sendero rifle is the most accurate rifle Remington produces for over-the-counter sale. You'll be stunned by the degree of precision you get straight out of the box. The H.S. Precision composite stock is reinforced and features a contoured beavertail fore-end with ambidextrous finger grooves and palm swell. Full-length aluminum bedding blocks provide an accuracy-enhancing platform for the action. The 26" heavy-contour barrel is fluted for rapid cooling.

Backcountry hunting demands high standards, that's where the Model 700™ Ti. Weighing only 6 1/4 pounds long action and 6 pounds short action – it's the ultimate rifle for high-altitude spot-and-stalk hunting. The key to the lightweight feel starts with a titanium receiver that's impervious to weather, incredibly strong, and half the weight of steel.

The Remington 700 CDL is about as classic of a big game hunting rifle as you can get these days. Graceful lines, attention to detail and legendary accuracy make these rifles solid investments.

With the Model 700 XCR, Remington took everything we knew about a stainless steel rifle and reinvented it. That is due to the TriNyte® Corrosion Control System (Patent pending). Consisting of electroless nickel and proprietary PVD, this armor-tough, multi-layer coating is the world's most effective barrier against rust and abrasion for firearms.

Gerber

www.gergear.com

From skinning knives to the ever-useful multi-tool, Gerber has all your cutting, chopping and skinning needs covered.

Traverse: 3 1/8" stainless steel 7Cr17 blade, dual Thumbstuds-one handed knife, lightweight aluminum handle with pocket clip.

The Gerber Automatic: The Gerber Automatic has an oversized release button, which can be really handy when you're wearing gloves. The blade is premium stainless steel and holds an edge. Having a good, sharp knife is a vital part of hunting.

Stealthcam

www.stealthcam.net

For remote scouting, game cameras can be a valuable asset; Stealthcam makes some of the best, innovative products in their category.

The Stealthcam Prowler is as high-tech as you can get in a digital game camera. It features 5 MP resolution for daytime images and 2MP black and white night time images. The infrared flash illuminates out to 50 feet yet doesn't spook game.

Cyclops Headlamps and Flashlights

www.cyclopssolutions.com

A good flashlight and headlamp are indispensable for the backcountry hunter; choose from many models with Cyclops.

The Cyclops Helios has six LED bulbs, a two-way switch, is water resistant and very lightweight. They even include the batteries!

Mountain House

www.mountainhouse.com

While not as good as home cooking, Mountain House freeze-dried foods are the best I have found for wilderness meals.

Wilderness Athlete

www.wildernessathlete.org

Specializing in high performance nutritional products for backcountry hunters, Wilderness Athlete will keep you going that extra mile.

My Topo

www.mytopo.com

This is an excellent site for researching areas or printing custom topographical maps for use in the field.

Whether you're pouring over it prior to heading out, or looking things over while in the field, a good map is a vital link between where you are and where you want to be. My Topo allows you to customize your map to your needs on a waterproof map that will withstand the elements.

Delorme Maps

www.delorme.com

With general public land and public hunting and fishing areas marked as well as topo and roads, this is my first "go to" map when I start looking for backcountry areas to hunt.

Delorme has long been known for making top quality maps and mapping software. They also produce a high-quality handheld GPS unit that comes loaded with their latest software. The Earthmate GPS PN-20 is one of the best mapping GPS units you can get!

Brunton

www.brunton.com

This is one of my favorite backcountry manufacturers. Originally a compass company, and while they still produce excellent compasses, they make a myriad of backcountry applicable products from tiny stoves and lanterns to optics and solar chargers.

The Conventional compass from Brunton uses Alnico II magnets and a "V" cut sapphire jewel bearing for smooth movement. Conventional suspension offers premium performance. The body is diecast aluminum, making the Conventional not only accurate, but also durable, a very important element of backcountry gear.

The Brunton Polaris is the first LED lantern to have a natural light instead of the typical glaring, white LED we're used to. It also gives you 360 degrees of light with no dead spots. The Polaris emits a warm orange glow similar to a propane lantern with mantle.

Garmin GPS

www.garmin.com

GPS units are so common afield it is hard to imagine what early explorers did without them. While there are many available, I prefer Garmin because they do everything I need, and are simple to use even for someone who is not ultra-tech savvy.

The Garmin eTrex series of handheld GPS units offer everything a sportsperson would need: accuracy, dependability, and simplicity. These waterproof units last up to 17 hours of continuous running time and fit in your pocket.

One of the smallest and lightest GPS units available, the Garmin Geko 301 has the accuracy and dependability you'd want. This unit also has a built-in electronic compass and a barometric altimeter that can provide crucial information should you need it. Not only do barometric changes effect game movements, they also can predict weather changes.

IMMERSE YOURSELF IN HUNTING HERITAGE AND HOW-TO'S

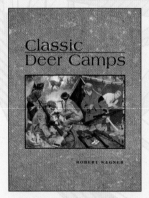